PILGRIM'S PROGRESS

Pilgrim's Progress

From this world to that which is to come

John Bunyan

Edited by Rhona Pipe

HODDER &
STOUGHTON

British Library Cataloguing in Publication Data
A record for this book is available from the British Library

ISBN 0 340 38171 X

Printed and bound in Great Britain by
Clays Ltd, St Ives plc

The paper and board used in this paperback are natural recyclable
products made from wood grown in sustainable forests.
The manufacturing processes conform to the environmental
regulations of the country of origin.

Hodder and Stoughton
A Division of Hodder Headline Ltd
338 Euston Road
London NW1 3BH

www.madaboutbooks.com

Contents

Introduction

JOHN BUNYAN

John Bunyan was born in the village of Elstow, near Bedford, in 1628. He died in August 1688, and was buried in Bunhill Fields, London. His father was a tinker, and John Bunyan learned the common trade of mending pots and pans. What a humble start in life for the man who became 'one of the great figures of the Reformation, a valiant fighter for truth, a preacher and a pastor, and the author of one of the best-selling books in the history of English literature.'[1]

Although Bunyan's parents were poor, he was sent to school where he was taught to read and write, and Bunyan saw the providential hand of God in that. From the early age of 9 Bunyan was tormented with horrific dreams and visions about his own guilt, about hell and the impossibility of attaining heaven. As he grew up, however, Bunyan became so prolific at swearing and so confirmed in his habit of cursing that in one of his more reflective moments he said, 'I wished with all my heart that I might be a little child again.' A woman, who was far from being godly herself, once openly rebuked Bunyan for his foul language, and this had an amazing effect! It stopped Bunyan in his tracks and set in motion a most unexpected turnabout in his life. In later years Bunyan commented that during this time of his outward moral reformation 'he knew neither Christ, nor grace nor faith.' Yet at that stage in his life Bunyan congratulated himself on being a religious man who pleased God. Then this self-confidence was dented when he met three godly women who talked to him about their own righteousness being worthless in God's sight.

At the age of 19 Bunyan's sources for his Christian enlightenment were the Bible and the Holy Spirit. He had virtually no human guides at this time in his life. He became ardent in his painstaking study of the Bible as he sought to satisfy his hungry soul with the rich spiritual truths about eternal life and God's forgiveness.

Eventually Bunyan shared his spiritual quest with those three Christian women who had originally made such an impression on him. They introduced him to John Gifford, a godly Baptist minister, who became to Bunyan what Evangelist became to Pilgrim in *Pilgrim's Progress*. The initial result of his conversations with John Gifford surprised and at the time upset him. His eyes were opened to the deep-seated evil desires of his own heart so that he was almost drowned by the reality of his own wickedness. This onerous burden lifted when he heard a sermon about the love of Christ. So at the age of 25, in a quiet Bedford field, Bunyan was baptised by John Gifford.

But Bunyan's spiritual struggles, if anything, continued to intensify. The experience of being in the grip of terrifying demons, and the invasion of wave upon wave of darkness into his soul, made Bunyan believe that he was on the edge of insanity.

An old dog-eared copy of Martin Luther's *Commentary on Galatians* was used by God to deliver Bunyan out of his own very real Slough of Despond. As he read Luther, Bunyan felt that he could have been reading his own spiritual autobiography. Luther had written about his tremendous fear of eternal damnation before going on to explain that the way of escape came solely through God's mercy. Bunyan's soul was flooded with spiritual light. His fevered brain cooled as he took comfort from this reassuring truth. After the Bible, Luther's book was Bunyan's treasure. (Many writers on Bunyan point out that Bunyan hardly read or referred to any other book except the Bible, apart from his love for Luther's *Commentary on Galatians* and Fox's *History of the Martyrs*.)

Power for the people

Then, quite out of the blue, Bunyan discovered that he had been given a special gift to speak and to preach in such a way that ordinary people could both understand and respond to. Robert Browning agreed:

> A fiery tear he put in tone.
> 'Tis my belief God spoke; no tinker has such powers.

The learned Dr John Owen, famed for his own writings, who with Richard Baxter was the most eminent Dissenter of the time, was once reproved by King Charles II for going to listen to 'that illiterate tinker prate'. Owen replied to the king, 'Please, your majesty, could I possess that tinker's abilities for preaching, I would gladly relinquish all my learning.' Dr George Wheeler in his 'Introductory Memoir' to his 1851 edition of *Pilgrim's Progress* comments on this incident.

> Owen was right, and the anecdote is exceedingly to his credit; for Bunyan's abilities for preaching, Owen knew well, resulted from the teachings and influences of the Holy Spirit, without which all human learning, even in God's Word, would be vain; and moreover, Bunyan's abilities for preaching were precisely the same gifts of incomparable genius and piety that produced *Pilgrim's Progress*.

Power outburst from prison

A small group of people sat with their Bibles open listening to Bunyan preach in a farmhouse in Lower Samsell. Suddenly men burst in and had Bunyan taken away and thrown into prison. It led to Bunyan's being in prison for almost all the next twelve years. Before Justice Keelin, Bunyan's famous reply was, 'If I were out of prison today, I would preach the gospel again tomorrow, by the help of God.' In the turbulent days after the English Civil War, Parliament issued the 1662 Act of Uniformity, decreeing that all churches had to use the Prayer Book. Along with 2,000 other Puritans, Bunyan was dismissed from his living and soon found himself locked in a damp prison cell for holding open-air 'non-conformist' worship services. *Pilgrim's Progress* was the fruit of Bunyan's imprisonment.

Bunyan was released from prison on May 9th, 1672, and as Offor noted, on the form of the royal sanction was the memorable fact that Bunyan's licensure was 'the first permission to preach given to any Dissenter from the established sect in this country.' Bunyan himself wrote of his imprisonment as a time when 'I never had in all my life so great an inlet into the Word of God as now. Jesus Christ also was never made more real and apparent than now; because I have seen and felt him indeed.'

Bunyan became a much appreciated pastor and preacher in Bedford. On page lxxxiv of his *Introductory Memoir of the Author of Pilgrim's Progress* Dr Cheever writes,

> During these last years of his life, and indeed from the time of his release out of prison, and his entrance on the full responsibility of his pastorship, to the period of his death, Bunyan's labours, both as a preacher and a writer, were incessant and exceedingly great. He mingled the vocations of a pastor and an author more successfully and laboriously than any other man except Baxter. 'Here's sixty pieces of his labours,' Charles Doe quaintly remarks, at the end of the catalogue of his books published and unpublished; 'and he was sixty years of age.'

Bunyan's final sermon, at the age of 59, on the appropriate theme of Christians' loving each other (during a time of bitter sectarianism among Christians) was in a meeting-house near Whitechapel. On the way there he was drenched by rain. He subsequently fell ill with pneumonia from which he died on August 31st, 1688.

Pilgrim's Progress

Pilgrim's Progress, which has been such a source of inspiration for 300 years, and a gold-mine of arresting illustrations for generations of preachers, simply tells the story of the spiritual pilgrimage of Christian from his City of Destruction to the Celestial City. Christian's joys, struggles, temptations, distractions and dangers are displayed through his meetings with characters such as Pliable, Talkative, Giant Despair, Worldly-Wiseman, Evangelist, Apollyon, Faithful (who is martyred in Vanity Fair), Hopeful and Ignorance.

It would not be difficult to collect reams of quotations which applaud Bunyan for his inimitable *Pilgrim's Progress*.

> … his mastery of plain yet often beautiful and rhythmical English prose, his powerful insight and keen observation of contemporary life, and above all his imagination and heroic spirit have given *Pilgrim's Progress* … a permanent place among the English classics.'[2]

> It is my conviction that *Pilgrim's Progress* is incomparably the best 'Summa Theologiae evangelicae' ever produced by a writer not miraculously inspired (S.T. Coleridge).

> The truth is that *The Pilgrim's Progress* is one of the rare works which give man his measure – his weak-

nesses, his imperfections, his meanness, but also his
will, his courage and his thirst for the absolute.
Bunyan does not confine himself to one extremity but
he touches both at the same time, and in that lies the
best testimony to his genius.[3]

Bunyan is one of the few original men who have
been given to the church (J.A. Ken Bain, DD).

But Bunyan did not write *Pilgrim's Progress* for literary
accolades. His simple straightforward style earned him
little respect from contemporary literary figures. Bunyan
wrote to encourage and teach fellow-Christians on their
spiritual pilgrimage. Countless thousands have thanked
God with all their hearts for this tinker of Bedford.

Edition to mark the 300th anniversary of Bunyan's death

This edition was published to mark the 300th anninversary
of Bunyan's death. The text is unabridged and follows the
1678 edition of *Pilgrim's Progress*. All the names of the
characters Christian meets have been retained, as have the
names of the places Christian visits, and Bunyan's sections
of poetry have also been left unaltered.

Changes have been made to Bunyan's words and phrases
where the seventeenth-century language and rhythms
obscure his meaning for late twentieth-century readers.
The aim has been to communicate the exact meaning of
Bunyan, in down-to-earth language for people today,
where Bunyan wrote in down-to-earth language for people
of his day. The text is no longer set out like a play, as in the
1678 edition, but the passages of dialogue are written in the
way to which we are now accustomed.

This edition ends by including Bunyan's original 'Conclusion' to *Pilgrim's Progress*, but it does not include a work

Bunyan subsequently wrote as a sequel which is now known as *The Second Part of the Pilgrim*. In that part Christian's wife, Christiana, and her children, follow in Christian's footsteps, meeting the same people he met, in their journey from the City of Destruction to the Celestial City.

In the 1678 edition no chapter divisions were indicated, but following common practice, this edition has inserted chapters. The sub-headings of this edition are Bunyan's original ones. Readers who wish to see Bunyan's old English spelling and original layout will find it interesting to look at Oxford University Press's edition of *Bunyan. Grace Abounding and The Pilgrim's Progress*, edited by Roger Sharrock. This book shows how Bunyan used to group Bible references in the margin and link them to particular words by means of asterisks.

This present edition includes all of Bunyan's many Bible references, using the New Internationl Version of the Bible. Where Bunyan quotes or refers to Bible passages, but did not give the Bible reference, these are now supplied. (It would appear that Bunyan's first readers were more familiar with their Bibles than many contemporary readers are, who would be hard-pressed to know where people like Topheth, Gehezi, Hymenaeus or Philetus come in the Bible, or what they signify!) This edition has two indexes, a general index and an index of Bible references.

Pilgrim's Progress can be read on many levels

The story of Christian's adventurous journey to the Celestial City makes an absorbing read in itself. For those familiar with this book it can be reread with great profit for its rich spiritual counsel and incisive Biblical insights. One way to do this would be to look up every Bible reference, read and meditate on each one. The first batch of references in Chapter 1, for example, refer to the passage

I saw a man clothed in rags. He stood with his face away

from his own house, a book in his hand, and a great burden on his back. I looked, and saw him open the book,
and read it, and as he read he wept and trembled.
Unable to contain himself, he broke down with a
heartbreaking cry, calling out, 'What shall I do?' (Isa.
64:6; Luke 14:33; Ps. 38:4; Hab. 2:2; Acts 2:37).

The first Bible reference here is Isaiah, chapter 64, verse
6, which reads, 'All of us have become like one who is unclean, and all our righteous acts are like filthy rags; we all
shrivel up like a leaf, and like the wind our sins sweep us
away.' From this it is clear that when he refers to a man
'clothed in rags' Bunyan is making a point about the sad
spiritual state of those who live in the City of Destruction.
In the same way, Psalm 38, verse 4, elucidates Bunyan's
reference to the 'great burden' Christian had on his back.

Pilgrim's Progress is a great book for those who are
thinking about how to start out on their spiritual pilgrimage, or having recently started, wonder what is going to
face them. But it is also really encouraging to Christians
who are bogged down in their own spiritual Slough of
Despond or trapped and racked by their own doubts in the
dungeon of Doubting Castle. Those who worry about
dying, or who are facing the imminent prospect of death,
can derive immense comfort and hope as they read the last
chapter of *Pilgrim's Progress* and see how it pictures the last
step of their own spiritual pilgrimage before they are welcomed by the King of the Celestial City.

Macaulay pointed out that *Pilgrim's Progress* 'is the only
book of its kind that possesses a strong human interest, that
while other allegories only amuse the fancy, this has been
read by thousands with tears.'[4] John Brown goes on to write,

   It not merely gives pleasure to the intellect by its wit
   and ingenuity, it gets hold of the heart by its life-grip.
   With deepest pathos it enters into that stern battle so
   real to all of us, into those heart-experiences which

make up for all the discipline of life. It is this especially which has given to it the mighty hold which it always had upon the toiling poor, and made it the one book above all books, well thumbed and worn to tatters among them ... He who is nearest to the Bible is nearest to the *Pilgrim's Progress* in its comprehensive Christ-like spirit.[5]

Notes

1 Stuart Blanch, in his Foreword to *He Shall With Giants Fight*, Anne Arnott (Kingsway, 1985), p.7.
2 Vivian de Sola Pinto, in *Chambers Encyclopaedia*.
3 Henri Talon, *John Bunyan, the Man and his Works* (Rockliff, 1951), p.224.
4 *John Bunyan: His Life, Times and Work,* John Brown (Isbister, 1885), p.299.
5 Ibid.

Halcyon Backhouse

The Author's *Apology* for his Book

When at the first I took my pen in hand,
Thus for to write, I did not understand
That I at all should make a little book
In such a mode: nay, I had undertook
To make another; which, when almost done,
Before I was aware, I thus begun.

And thus it was: I, writing of the way
And race of saints in this our gospel-day,
Fell suddenly into an allegory
About their journey and the way to glory,
In more than twenty things, which I set down:
This done, I twenty more had in my crown;
And then again began to multiply,
Like sparks that from the coals of fire do fly.
Nay then, thought I, if that you breed so fast,
I'll put you by yourselves, lest you at last
Should prove *ad infinitum*, and eat out
The book that I already am about.

Well, so I did; but yet I did not think
To show to all the world my pen and ink
In such a mode; I only thought to make I knew not what;
    nor did I undertake
Thereby to please my neighbour; no, not I;
I did it mine own self to gratify.

Neither did I but vacant seasons spend
In this my scribble; nor did I intend
But to divert myself, in doing this,
From worser thoughts, which make me do amiss.

Thus I set pen to paper with delight,
And quickly had my thoughts in black and white,
For having now my method by the end,
Still as I pull'd, it came; and so I penn'd
It down; until at last it came to be,
For length and breadth, the bigness which you see.

Well, when I had thus put my ends together,
I showed them others, that I might see whether
They would condemn them, or them justify;
And some said, Let them live; some, Let them die:
Some said, John, print it; others said, Not so:
Some said, It might do good; others said, No.

Now was I in a strait, and did not see
Which was the best thing to be done by me:
At last I thought, Since you are thus divided,
I print it will; and so the case decided.
For, thought I, some I see would have it done,
Though others in that channel do not run:
To prove, then, who advisèd for the best,
Thus I thought fit to put it to the test.

I further thought, if now I did deny
Those that would have it thus to gratify,
I did not know, but hinder them I might
Of that which would to them be great delight:
For those which were not for its coming forth,
I said to them, *Offend you I am loth*;
Yet, since your brethren pleasèd with it be,
Forbear to judge, till you do further see.

If that you will not read, let it alone;
Some love the meat, some love to pick the bone;
Yea, that I might them better moderate,
I did too with them thus expostulate:

May I not write in such a style as this?
In such a method, too, and yet not miss
My end, thy good? Why may it not be done?

Dark clouds bring waters, when the bright bring none.
Yea, dark or bright, if they their silver drops
Cause to descend, the earth, by yielding crops,
Gives praise to both, and carpeth not at either,
But treasures up the fruit they yield together;
Yea, so commixes both, that in their fruit
None can distinguish this from that; they suit
Her well when hungry; but if she be full,
She spews out both, and makes their blessing null.

You see the ways the fisherman doth take
To catch the fish; what engines doth he make.
Behold! how he engageth all his wits;
Also his snarers, lines, angles, hooks, and nets:
Yet fish there be, that neither hook nor line,
Nor snare, nor net, nor engine, can make thine:
They must be groped for, and be tickled too,
Or they will not be catch'd, whate'er you do.
How does the fowler seek to catch his game?
By divers means, all which one cannot name:
His guns, his nets, his lime-twigs, light, and bell;
He creeps, he goes, he stands; yea, who can tell
Of all his postures? Yet there's none of these
Will make him master of what fowls he please.
Yea, he must pipe and whistle to catch this,
Yet, if he does so, that bird he will miss.

If that a pearl may in a toad's head dwell,
And may be found, too, in an oyster-shell:
If things that promise nothing do contain
What better is than gold, who will disdain,
That have an inkling of it, there to look,
That they may find it? Now, my little book
(Though void of all these paintings that may make
It with this or the other man to take)
Is not without those things that do excel
What do in brave but empty notions dwell.

Well, yet I am not fully satisfied,
That this your book will stand when soundly tried.

Why, what's the matter? *It is dark!* What though?
But it is feigned. What of that, I trow?
Some men, by feignèd words, as dark as mine,
Make truth to spangle, and its rays to shine!
But they want solidness. Speak, man, thy mind!
They drown the weak; metaphors make us blind.

Solidity, indeed, becomes the pen
Of him that writeth things divine to men:
But must I needs want solidness, because
By metaphors I speak? Were not God's laws,
His gospel laws, in olden time held forth
By shadows, types, and metaphors? Yet loth
Will any sober man be to find fault
With them, lest he be found for to assault
The highest Wisdom. No, he rather stoops,
And seeks to find out what by pins and loops,
By Calves, and Sheep; by Heifers, and by Rams;
By Birds and Herbs, and by the blood of Lambs;
God speaketh to him: And happy is he
That finds the light, and grace that in them be.

Be not too forward therefore to conclude,
That I want solidness; that I am rude:
All things solid in shew, not solid be;
All things in parables despise not we,
Lest things most hurtful lightly we receive;
And things that good are, of our souls bereave.

My dark and cloudy words they do but hold
The Truth, as Cabinets inclose the Gold.

The Prophets used much by metaphors
To set forth Truth; Yea, who so considers
Christ, his Apostles too, shall plainly see,
That Truths to this day in such Mantles be.

Am I afraid to say that holy Writ,

Which for its stile, and phrase, puts down all wit,
Is every where so full of all these things,
(Dark figures, allegories) yet there springs
From that same Book that lustre, and those rayes
Of light, that turns our darkest nights to days.

Come, let my Carper, to his Life now look,
And find there darker lines, than in my Book
He findeth any. Yea, and let him know,
That in his best things there are worse lines too.

May we but stand before impartial men,
To his poor One, I durst adventure Ten,
That they will take my meaning of these lines
Far better then his lies in Silver Shrines.
Come, Truth, although in Swadling-clouts, I find
Informs the Judgement, rectifies the Mind,
Pleases the Understanding, makes the Will
Submit; the Memory too it doth fill
With what doth our Imagination please;
Likewise, it tends our troubles to appease.

Sound words I know *Timothy* is to use;
And old Wives Fables he is to refuse,
But yet grave *Paul* him no where doth forbid
The use of parables; in which lay hid
That God, those Pearls, and precious stones that were
Worth digging for; and that with greatest care.

Let me add one word more, O Man of God!
Art thou offended? does thou wish I had
Put forth my matter in another dress,
Or that I had in things been more express?
Three things let me propound, then I submit
To those that are my betters (as is fit).

1. I find not that I am denied the use
Of this my method, so I no abuse
Put on the Words, Things, Readers, or be rude
In handling Figure, or Similitude,

In application; but, all that I may,
Seek the advance of Truth, this or that way:
Denyed did I say? Nay, I have leave,
(Example too, and that from them that have
God better pleased by their words or ways,
Then any Man that breatheth now adays,)
Thus to express my mind, thus to declare
Things unto thee that excellentest are.

2. I find that men (as high as Trees) will write
Dialogue-wise; yet no Man doth them slight
For writing so: Indeed if they abuse
Truth, cursed be they, and the craft they use
To that intent; but yet let Truth be free
To make her Salleys upon Thee, and Me,
Which way it pleases God. For who knows how,
Better then he that taught us first to Plow,
To guide our Mind and Pens for his Design?
And he makes base things usher in Divine.

3. I find that holy Writ in many places,
Hath semblance with this method, where the cases
Doth call for one thing to set forth another:
Use it I may then, and yet nothing smother
Truths golden Beams; Nay, by this method may
Make it cast forth its rayes as light as day.

And now, before I do put up my Pen,
I'le shew the profit of my Book, and then
Commit both thee, and it unto that hand
That pulls the strong down, and makes weak ones stand.

This Book it chaulketh out before thine eyes,
The man that seeks the everlasting Prize:
It shews you whence he comes, whither he goes,
What he leaves undone; also what he does:
It also shews you how he runs, and runs,
Till he unto the Gate of Glory comes.

It shews too, who sets out for life amain,

As if the lasting Crown they would attain:
Here also you may see the reason why
They loose their labour, and like fools do die.

This Book will make a Travailer of thee,
If by its Counsel thou wilt ruled be;
It will direct thee to the Holy Land,
If thou wilt its directions understand:
Yea, it will make the sloathful, active be;
The blind also, delightful things to see.

Art thou for something rare, and profitable?
Wouldest thou see a Truth within a fable?
Art thou forgetful? Wouldest thou remember
From *New-years-day* to the last of *December*?
Then read my fancies, they will stick like burs,
And may be to the Helpless, comforters.

This book is writ in such a dialect,
As may the minds of listless men affect:
It seems a novelty, and yet contains
Nothing but sound and honest Gospel-strains.

Wouldst thou divert thy self from Melancholly?
Would'st thou be pleasant, yet be far from folly?
Would'st thou read riddles, and their explanation,
Or else be drownded in thy Contemplation?
Dost thou love picking-meat? or would'st thou see
A man i' the clouds, and hear him speak to thee?
Would'st thou be in a Dream, and yet not sleep?
Or would'st thou in a moment laugh and weep?
Wouldest thou loose thy self, and catch no harm?
And find thy self again without a charm?
Would'st read thy self, and read thou know'st not what
And yet know whether thou art blest or not,
By reading the same lines? O then come hither,
And lay my Book, thy Head and Heart together.

JOHN BUNYAN

THE PILGRIM'S PROGRESS:

In the similitude of a dream

1

The Hollow and the Dreamer

Walking through the wilderness of this world I came upon a place where there was a hollow (the gaol). There I lay down to sleep: and as I slept I dreamed a dream. I dreamed, and look! I saw a man clothed with rags. He stood with his face away from his own house, a book in his hand, and a great burden on his back. I looked, and saw him open the book, and read it. As he read he wept and trembled. Unable to contain himself, he broke down with a heartbreaking cry, calling out, 'What shall I do?' (Isa. 64:6; Luke 14:33; Ps. 38:4; Hab. 2:2; Acts 2:37). And in this state he went home. Here he held himself back for as long as he could so that his wife and children shouldn't see his distress. But he couldn't be silent for long because his trouble grew worse. Finally he unburdened himself to his wife and children. 'My dear wife,' he said, 'and you children of my deepest love, I, your dear friend, feel utterly crushed under a burden too heavy to bear. The worst of it is, I have sure information that this city of ours will be burned with fire from heaven. In this dreadful destruction, both I, and you, my wife, and you my sweet babies, will be miserably destroyed unless we find some way of escape. But as yet I can see none.'

At this his family were very distressed, not because they believed that what he said to them was true, but because they thought that some madness had got into his head. As it was drawing towards night and they hoped that sleep might settle his mind, they hastily got him to bed. But the night was as troublesome to him as the day. And instead of sleeping he spent it in sighs and tears.

When morning came they wanted to know how he was and he told them, 'It's worse and worse.' He also set about talking to them again. But they began to grow hard. They thought that a harsh, surly attitude would drive away this derangement. Sometimes they derided, sometimes they scolded, and sometimes they totally neglected him. As a result he began to withdraw to his own room to pray for and pity them, and also to grieve over his misery. He began to walk by himself in the fields, sometimes reading and sometimes praying. For some days he spent his time in this way.

Now one day he was walking in the fields reading his book as usual, and feeling greatly distressed, when he burst out, as he had done before, with the cry, 'What must I do to be saved?' (Acts 16:30). He looked one way and then the other as if he wanted to run. Yet he stood still and I saw that this was because he couldn't tell which way to run.

Then I saw a man coming to him whose name was Evangelist. He asked, 'Why are you crying?'

'Sir,' he answered, 'I understand from this book I'm holding that I'm condemned to die and after that to face judgment (Heb. 9:27); and I find that I'm not willing to do the first (Job 16:21–22), nor able to do the second' (Ezek. 22.14).

Evangelist then said, 'Why aren't you willing to die, since this life has so many evils?'

The man answered, 'Because I'm afraid that this burden on my back will sink me lower than the grave, and I'll fall into Topheth (Isa. 30:33). And, sir, if I'm unfit to go to prison I'm certainly not fit to go to judgment, and from there to execution. It's the thought of all these things that makes me cry.'

Conviction of the necessity of fleeing

Then Evangelist said, 'If this is your condition, why are you standing still?'

He answered, 'Because I don't know where to go.'

Then Evangelist gave him a parchment in which was written, 'Flee from the coming wrath' (Matt. 3:7).

Christ and the way to him cannot be found without the word

So the man read it, and looking at Evangelist very carefully he said, 'Where must I flee to?'

Then Evangelist pointed with his finger over a very wide field. 'Do you see that distant wicket-gate?' he asked (Matt. 7:14).

The man said, 'No.'

'Well, do you see that shining light in the distance?' (Ps. 119:105; 2 Pet. 1:19).

'I think I do.'

Then Evangelist said, 'Keep that light in your eye and go straight towards it. Then you'll see the gate. When you knock on it you'll be told what to do.'

So in my dream I saw that the man began to run. But he hadn't run far from his own door when his wife and children saw him and began to cry out to him to return (Luke 14:26). But the man put his fingers in his ears and ran on crying, 'Life! Life! Eternal life!' He didn't look back, but fled towards the middle of the plain (Gen. 19:17).

Those who flee from the coming wrath are a spectacle to the world

The neighbours too came out to see the man run. Some mocked (Jer. 20:10) as he ran, others threatened, and some implored him to return. Among all these there were some who resolved to fetch him back by force.

Obstinate and Pliable follow him

One was named Obstinate and the other Pliable. Now by this time the man was a good distance from them, but, they were determined to pursue him, and in a little while they overtook him.

Then the man said, 'Why have you come, friends?'

They said, 'To persuade you to go back with us.'

But he said, 'No! That's impossible. I know you live in the city of Destruction, the place where I was born. Sooner or later you'll die there and you'll sink lower than the grave to a place that burns with fire and sulphur. You're good neighbours, be content to come along with me.'

'What!' said Obstinate, 'and leave our friends? Leave all our comforts behind us!'

'Yes,' said Christian, for that was the man's name, 'because what you're leaving isn't worth half of what I'm seeking to enjoy (2 Cor. 4:18). And if you do go along with me and don't give up, you'll fare as well as I do, for where I'm going there's enough and to spare (Luke 15:17). Come on. Prove it.'

'What are these things, you're leaving all the world for?' asked Obstinate.

'I seek an "inheritance that can never perish, spoil or fade" (1 Pet. 1:4), "it's kept in heaven", safe there, ready to be given at the appointed time to everyone who looks hard for it. (Heb. 11:16). Read about it, if you want, in the book.'

'Rubbish!' said Obstinate. 'Get away with your book! Will you go back with us or not?'

'No, not me, because I've put my hand to the plough' (Luke 9:62).

'Right, then. Come on, Pliable, let's turn back and go

home without him. We're in the company of one of those crazy-headed jackasses who gets hold of a whim and in the end thinks he's wiser than seven sane men.'

Then Pliable said, 'Don't be so abusive. If what Christian says is true, the things he's seeking are better than ours. I'm inclined to go with my neighbour.'

'What! Even more of a fool!' exclaimed Obstinate. 'Take my advice. Come on back. Who knows where someone so sick in the head will lead you? Show a bit of sense and come back.'

Christian and Obstinate pull for Pliable's soul

'No, come with me, Pliable,' Christian urged. 'There really are such things for us to possess and many more splendours besides. If you don't believe me, read for yourself here in this book. Its truth is guaranteed by the blood of the one who made it. Look!' (Heb. 9:17–21).

Pliable consents to go with Christian

'Well, Obstinate,' said Pliable, 'I'm about to make a decision. I intend to go along with my friend here and cast in my lot with him. But, look here,' he said to Christian, 'do you know the way to this desirable place?'

'A man called Evangelist directed me to hurry on to a little gate just ahead of us,' Christian replied, 'where we'll be given instructions about the way.'

'Come on then,' said Pliable, 'let's get going.'

So they then both went on together.

'And I'll go back to my place,' said Obstinate. 'I'm not keeping company with such deluded maniacs.'

2

The Slough of Despond

Now in my dream I saw that when Obstinate had gone back Christian and Pliable went on over the plain, talking together.

Christian said, 'Well, Pliable. How're you, friend? I'm glad you decided to go along with me. If Obstinate had felt what I've felt of the powers and terrors of the unseen, he wouldn't have been so quick to turn his back on us.'

'Well then, Christian, as there's no one apart from us to hear, tell me more. What are these things you're on about? How can we enjoy them, and where are we going?'

'I can picture them in my mind, better than describe them with words. But even so, as you do want to know I'll read about them from my book.'

'And do you think that the words of your book are really true?'

'Oh yes, absolutely. Because it was made by the one who doesn't lie' (Titus 1:2).

'Well said! What are these things, Christian?'

'There's an everlasting kingdom to be inherited, and eternal life to be given us, that we may inhabit the kingdom for ever' (Isa. 45:17; John 10:27–9).

'Well said! And what else?'

'There are crowns of glory to be given us and clothes to make us shine like the sun in the firmament of heaven' (2 Tim. 4:8; Rev. 3:4; Matt. 13:43).

'This is splendid! And what else?'

'There will be no more crying nor sorrow, for the owner

of the place will wipe every tear from our eyes' (Isa. 25:8; Rev. 7:16–17, 21:4).

'And what sort of company shall we have there?'

'There we'll be with Seraphs and will see Cherubim – creatures that'll dazzle your eyes (Isa. 6:2; 1 Thess. 4:16–17; Rev. 5:11). There you'll also meet with thousands and ten thousands that have gone before us to that place. None of them is hurtful, but loving and holy; everyone walking in the sight of God, and standing in his presence, accepted by him for ever. There we'll see the elders with their golden crowns (Rev. 4:4); the holy virgins with their golden harps (Rev. 14:1–5); and men whom the world cut to pieces, men who were burnt in flames, eaten by beasts, drowned in seas, for the love that they bear to the Lord of the place. And they will all be well and clothed with immortality as with a garment' (John 12:25; 2 Cor. 4:2–4).

'Just listening to this thrills my heart. But are these things actually for us? How shall we get to take part in it all?'

'The Lord, the Governor of that country, has told us in this book. The gist of it is that if we really want to have it, he'll give it freely' (Isa. 55:1–2; John 6:37; 7:37; Rev. 21:6; 22:17).

'Well, my good friend, am I glad to hear all this! Come on, let's get a move on.'

'I can't go as fast as I'd like, because of this burden on my back.'

Now in my dream I saw that just as they had ended this conversation they approached a very miry bog that was in the middle of the plain, and since neither of them was paying attention they suddenly fell into it. The name of bog was the Slough of Despond. They wallowed in it for a time, badly covered with the mud and because of the burden that was on his back Christian began to sink.

Then Pliable said, 'Ha! Christian, where are you now?'

'To be honest,' said Christian, 'I don't know.'

Pliable began to feel indignant. Angrily he said to his companion, 'Is this the happiness you've talked about all this time? If we have such bad luck right from the word go, what can we expect between now and the end of our journey? If I get out of this alive you can possess that brave new world all by yourself.' And with that he gave a few desperate struggles and finally got out of the bog on the side nearest to his own house. So away he went, and Christian didn't see him again.

Christian was left to stumble about in the Slough of Despond all by himself. Even so, he struggled hard to reach the side which was farthest from his house and nearest to the wicket-gate. He managed this, but couldn't get out because of the burden on his back. But in my dream I saw a man called Help come up to him and ask him what he was doing down there.

'Sir,' said Christian, 'I was told to go this way by a man called Evangelist, who also directed me to that gate over there so that I might escape the coming disaster. As I was going there, I fell in here.'

'But why didn't you look for the steps?' asked Help.

'Fear pursued me so closely that I fled the nearest way, and fell in.'

Then Help said, 'Give me your hand.'

So Christian gave him his hand, and Help lifted him out, stood him on firm ground, and sent him on his way (Ps. 40:2).

Then I stepped up to the man who had lifted Christian out, and said, 'Sir, since it is on the way from the City of Destruction to the gate over there, why is it that this bog is not filled in so that the poor travellers can get to the gate more safely?'

And he said to me, 'This miry bog is the kind of place that can't be repaired: all the scum and filth that accompany conviction for sin run endlessly down into it. So it's called the Slough of Despond. Whenever a sinner wakes up to his lost condition many fears and doubts rise up in his soul, many discouraging worries, all of which get together and settle in this place. And this is the reason for the bad state of this ground.

'It's not the king's wish that this place should remain so bad (Isa. 35:3–4). His labourers, under the direction of his majesty's surveyors, have been employed for more than these sixteen hundred years on this patch of ground to see if perhaps it might be improved. Yet, to my knowledge,' he continued, 'it has swallowed up at least twenty thousand cartloads, indeed millions, of wholesome instructions which have been brought in all seasons from all over the king's dominions to try and mend it. And those who know say they are the best possible materials for restoring the ground. But it is still the Slough of Despond. And so it will be when they have done all they can.'

The price of forgiveness and acceptance of life by faith in Christ

'At the direction of the Lawgiver, some good strong steps have been placed through the very middle of the bog, Help continued. 'But whenever this place spews out its filth – as it does when the weather changes – these steps can hardly be seen. Or if they are seen, in the dizziness of their heads, men step aside, and are then bogged down despite the steps. But the ground is good once they've got in at the gate' (1 Sam. 12:23).

Now in my dream I saw that by this time Pliable had reached home. So his neighbours came to visit him. Some of them called him wise for coming back; some called him a fool for risking his life in the first place; again, others mocked his cowardliness. 'Surely,' they said, 'since you began the venture … I wouldn't have been so base as to have given up because of a few difficulties!' So Pliable sat skulking among them. But at last he got his confidence back, and then they all changed their tune and began to deride poor Christian behind his back.

So much for Pliable.

3

Worldly-Wiseman

Now as Christian was walking all alone he spotted someone
far off, coming over the fields towards him, and it so happened that their paths crossed. The gentleman's name was
Mr Worldly-Wiseman and he lived in the town of Carnal-
Policy, a very great town, not far from where Christian
came from. This man had some inkling of who Christian
was, for news of Christian's departure from the City of
Destruction had been talked about a great deal. He had
heard of Christian not only in the town where he lived, but
also because he was the talk of the town in other places. So
Mr Worldly-Wiseman, having guessed it was Christian
from his laboured walk, and his sighs and groans, began to
talk to him.

Talk between Mr Worldly-Wiseman and Christian

'Hello my good man! Where're you off to in such a burdened state?' asked Mr Worldly-Wiseman.

'Burdened state indeed! As great, I think, as any poor
wretch has ever had to endure! And since you ask me, I'll
tell you, sir. I'm going to that wicket-gate over there ahead
of me. I'm told it's there that I'll be shown what to do about
my heavy burden.'

'Do you have a family – a wife and children?'

'Yes, but I'm so laden down with this burden that I can't
be happy with them as I used to be. I think I should live as

if I had none' (1 Cor 7:29).

'Will you listen to me if I give you some advice?'

'If it's good I will because I'm in need of some good advice.'

'I would advise you, then, to get rid of your burden as quickly as you can because you'll never be settled in your mind until you do. Nor will you be able to enjoy the benefits of the blessings God has given you.'

'That's exactly what I'm trying to do – to be rid of this heavy burden. But it's impossible for me to get it off myself. Nor is there a man in our country who can take it off my shoulders. That's why I'm going this way, as I told you, to be rid of my burden'.

'Who told you to go this way to get rid of it?'

'A man who seemed to me to be a very great and honourable person. His name, as I remember, is Evangelist.'

Mr Worldly-Wiseman condemns Evangelist's advice

'Curse him for his advice! There isn't a more dangerous and troublesome path in the world, as you'll find out if you do what he says. I notice you've encountered something already – I can see the filth of the Slough of Despond on you. That bog marks the beginning of the sorrows that accompany anyone who goes that way. Listen to me, I'm older than you. If you continue this way you're very likely to meet exhaustion, pain, hunger, danger, nakedness, sword, lions, dragons, darkness and, in a word, death, and who knows what else! These things are absolutely true. They've been confirmed by many witnesses. And why should a man carelessly throw himself away like that by paying attention to a stranger?'

The state of mind of young Christian

'Why, sir, this burden on my back is far worse than all these things you've mentioned. I feel as if I don't care what I meet on the way if I can also meet with deliverance from my burden.'

'How did you come by your burden in the first place?' asked Mr Worldly-Wiseman.

'By reading this book that I'm holding.'

'I thought so! The same thing has happened to other weak men. They go berserk through meddling with things too high for them. This madness not only unmans men (as I see it has done to you), but makes them run off on desperate ventures to get they know not what.'

'I know what I want; it's relief from my heavy burden.'

'But why seek relief in this way since it brings so many dangers, and especially since, if you'd only be patient and hear me out, I could show you how to get what you want without those dangers? Yes, the remedy is at hand. And, let me add, instead of those dangers you'll find safety, friendship and happiness.'

'Sir, let me in on this secret.'

Mr Worldly-Wiseman prefers Morality to the narrow gate

'Why, in that village over there, the one called Morality, a gentleman called Legality lives. He's a sensible type with a good reputation and has the ability to help men get rid of your kind of burden. Indeed, to my knowledge he's done a great deal of good in this way. Apart from this, he knows how to cure those people who are just about out of their mind with their burdens. As I said, you can go to him, and be quickly helped. His house isn't quite a mile from here, and if he's not at home himself, he has a good-looking son, called Civility, who can do what you want, come to that, as well as the old gentleman himself. That's where you can be eased of your burden, and if you don't feel like going back to your former way of life, as indeed I wouldn't wish you to, you can send for your wife and children, and settle in this village, where houses are standing empty right now. You could buy one at a reasonable price, and live well there, and cheaply. And to crown your happiness, you can be sure you'll live a respected and respectable life among honest neighbours, in good style, bringing credit to yourself.'

Now Christian was somewhat nonplussed by this. But soon he concluded that if what this gentleman had said was true, his wisest course of action would be to take his advice. And with that he went on: 'Sir, please direct me to this honest man's house. Which way is it?'

'Do you see that high hill over there?' (Mount Sinai)

'Yes, very clearly,' Christian said.

'Go by that hill and the first house you come to is his.'

Christian is afraid at Mount Sinai

So Christian turned off his course to go to Mr Legality's house for help. But when he got close to the hill it seemed too high. Furthermore, the side of the hill which was next to the road hung over so much that Christian was afraid to venture near in case the hill fell on his head. So he stood still, not knowing what to do. His burden, too, seemed heavier than when he had been on his course. And flashes of fire came out of the hill, which made Christian afraid that he would be burned (Exod. 19:16–18). He began to sweat and tremble with fear (Heb. 12:21).

Then just as Christian was feeling sorry that he had taken Mr Worldly-Wiseman's advice he saw Evangelist coming to meet him. At the sight of him Christian began to blush with shame. Evangelist drew closer and closer and coming right up to Christian looked at him with a severe and dreadful expression on his face. Then he began to reason with Christian.

'What can you hear, Christian?' Evangelist asked.

Christian didn't know how to reply to this, so he stood in silence.

Then Evangelist went on, 'Aren't you the man I found crying outside the walls of the City of Destruction?'

'Yes, dear sir, I am the man,' said Christian.

'Didn't I show you the way to the little wicket-gate?'

'Yes, dear sir,' said Christian.

'How is it, then, that you've turned away so quickly? You're well off course now.'

'Soon after I had got over the Slough of Despond I met a gentleman who persuaded me that I might find a man in the village ahead who could take off my burden.'

'What was he?'

'He looked like a gentleman. He talked a great deal and he finally got me to yield. So I came here. But when I saw this hill, and the way it hangs over the path, I stood stock-still in case it fell on my head.'

'What did that gentleman say to you?'

'He asked me where I was going, and I told him.'

'And what did he say then?'

'He asked me if I had a family, and I told him, but added that I'm so weighed down with this burden on my back that I can't be happy with them as I once was.'

'And what did he say then?'

'He urged me to get rid of my burden as quickly as possible. And I told him that was what I was seeking to do. I said, "This is why I'm going to that gate over there, to receive further instructions on how I can get to the place of deliverance." So he said he'd show me a better way. He said it was a shorter route, and one not so full of difficulties as the way you'd sent me on, sir. This way, he said, leads to the house of a gentleman who has the ability to take off these burdens. So I believed him. I turned out of that way into this in the hope that I might soon be rid of my burden. But when I came to the place, and saw things as they are, as I said, I stopped for fear of danger. And now I don't know what to do.'

Evangelist convinces Christian of his error

Then Evangelist said, 'Wait, while I show you the words of

God.' So Christian waited, trembling.

Then Evangelist said, 'Do not refuse him who warns you, for if they did not escape him who warned them on earth, how much less shall we escape if we turn away him who warns us from heaven?' (Heb. 12:25). In addition, he said, 'Now the just shall live by faith; but if he shrinks back, I will not be pleased with him' (Heb. 10:38).

Then he applied those words in this way: 'You're that man who is running into this misery. You've begun to reject the advice of the Most High and to draw back from the way of peace, almost risking your own destruction.'

Then Christian fell down at Evangelist's feet as if dead, and sobbed, 'God help me! I'm ruined!'

At this Evangelist caught him by the right hand and said, 'All the sins and blasphemies of men will be forgiven them; stop doubting and believe' (Matt. 12:31; John 20:27). Then Christian revived a little and stood up trembling, standing in front of Evangelist as before.

Evangelist went on, 'This time, pay more attention to what I tell you. I'm going to show you who it was who deluded you, and also who it was he sent you to. The man you met is someone called Worldly-Wiseman. He's rightly named, partly because he speaks only from the viewpoint of this world (1 John 4:5) – that's why he always goes to church in the town of Morality – and partly because he prefers his doctrine since it saves him from the cross (Gal. 6:12). So because he wants to create a good impression he seeks to turn people away from what I say, though it is right.'

Evangelist discloses the deceit of Mr Worldly-Wiseman

'Now there are three things about this man's advice which you must utterly hate.

'First, his turning you off the way.

'Second, his efforts to make the cross seem detestable.

'Third, his setting your feet on the road that leads to death.

'First, you must hate the way he turned you off course –
yes, and the way you agreed to it. You rejected the advice
of God, for the advice of a Worldly-Wiseman. The Lord
says, "Make every effort to enter through the narrow door"
(Luke 13:24) — the gate to which I send you; "For small is
the gate that leads to life, and only a few find it" (Matt.
7:14). This wicked man turned you away from this little wicket-gate, and from the path to it, bringing you almost to
destruction. So hate his turning you out of the way, and
hate yourself for listening to him.

'Second, you must loathe the way he works hard to make
the cross seem detestable. For you are to regard the cross as
of greater value than the treasures in Egypt (Heb. 11:26).
Besides, the king of glory has told you that the man who loves
his life will lose it; and anyone who comes after him and does
not hate his father and mother, his wife and children, his
brothers and sisters – yes, even his own life – cannot be my
disciple (Matt. 10:38; Mark 8:35; Luke 14.26; John 12.25).
So I say, you must utterly hate any doctrine which makes an
effort to persuade you that death will come through what, in
fact, the truth teaches is the only way you can have eternal life.

'Third, you must hate his setting your feet on the road that
leads to death.

'In addition, you must think about the man he sent you to.
Think how that man was completely unable to deliver you
from your burden. His name is Legality and he's the son of
the slave woman who lives in slavery with her children (Gal.
4:22–7). In a mysterous way, Legality is this Mount Sinai,
which you feared would fall on your head. Now if the woman
and her children are in slavery, how can you expect them to
set you free? This Legality is not able to set you free from
your burden. To this day no one has ever rid himself of his
burden through Legality nor is anyone ever likely to. By
observing the law no one will be justified, because by the
deeds of the law no man living can be rid of his burden.
Therefore Mr Worldly-Wiseman is an alien, and Mr Legality is a cheat. As for his son Civility, in spite of his affected

manner, he is merely a hypocrite, and certainly cannot help you. Believe me, all this blabber that you have heard from these stupid men is just designed to trick you out of your salvation by turning you from the way in which I set you.'

Then Evangelist called out loudly to the heavens to confirm what he'd said. Upon this, words and fire came out of the mountain under which poor Christian was standing, and made the hairs on his flesh stand on end. These were the words: 'All who rely on observing the law are under a curse, for it is written, "Cursed is everyone who does not continue to do everything written in the Book of the Law"' (Gal. 3:10).

Now Christian expected nothing but death and began to cry out bitterly. He cursed the day he met Mr Worldly-Wiseman, calling himself a thousand fools for listening to his advice. He was also terribly ashamed to think that this man's arguments, which stemmed only from the flesh, should have prevailed upon him and caused him to give up the right way. Then he turned his attention once again to Evangelist.

'Sir, what do you think? Is there any hope? May I retrace my steps and go on up to the wicket-gate? Won't I be abandoned, and sent back from there in disgrace? I'm sorry I've listened to this man's advice, but can my sin be forgiven?'

Evangelist comforts Christian

Then Evangelist said to him, 'Your sin is very great for through it you've committed two evils. You've forsaken the way that is good, and walked along a forbidden path. Yet the man at the gate will receive you, for he has goodwill towards men. Only beware of turning away again, lest you're destroyed on the way, for his wrath can flare up in a moment' (Ps. 2:12).

Then Christian set about returning, and Evangelist, after he had kissed him, smiled at him, and sent him off with God's blessing.

4

The Wicket-Gate

So Christian hurried on. He neither spoke to anyone on the way, nor, if anyone spoke to him, would he trust himself to give a reply. He journeyed like someone walking on forbidden ground. He didn't feel safe until he'd once again found the path which he'd left in order to follow Mr Worldly-Wiseman's advice.

So time passed and Christian arrived at the gate. Now above the gate were the words, 'Knock, and the door will be opened' (Matt. 7:8). So he knocked. He knocked a number of times, calling:

> May I now enter here? Will he within
> Open to sorry me, though I have bin
> An undeserving rebel? Then shall I
> Not fail to sing his lasting praise on high.

At last a person of authority – called Goodwill – came to the gate. Goodwill asked, 'Who's there? Where are you from? And what do you want?'

'This is a poor burdened sinner,' said Christian. 'I come from the City of Destruction, but I'm going to Mount Zion to be delivered from the wrath to come. Sir, I've been informed that the way there is through this gate, and I want to know if you're willing to let me in.'

The gate will be opened to broken-hearted sinners

'I am willing, with all my heart,' replied Goodwill, opening the gate.

As Christian was stepping in, Goodwill pulled him over the threshold. 'Why did you do that?' asked Christian.

Goodwill told him, 'A little way from this gate a strong castle has been built and Beelzebub is its captain. From there he and the others with him shoot arrows at those who come up here, hoping to kill them before they can get in.'

Then Christian said, 'I'm full of joy – and fear too.'

When Christian was safely in, the man at the gate asked who had directed him there.

'Evangelist told me to come here and knock as I did,' explained Christian. 'He also said that you, sir, would tell me what I must do.'

'An open door is before you which no one can shut,' said Goodwill.

So Christian said, 'Now I'm beginning to reap the benefits of the risks I've taken.'

'How is it that you came alone?' asked Goodwill.

'None of my neighbours saw their danger as I saw mine.'

'Did any of them know you were coming?'

'Yes, my wife and children saw me set off, and called after me to turn back. Also some of my neighbours stood crying, and calling to me to return. But I put my fingers in my ears, and hurried on.'

'But didn't anyone follow you to persuade you to go back?'

'Yes, two: Obstinate and Pliable. When they saw they couldn't succeed, Obstinate returned, ranting and railing, but Pliable came on with me a little way.'

'And why didn't he continue?'

'He did. Indeed both of us came on together until we reached the Slough of Despond, which we suddenly fell into. Then my neighbour Pliable felt discouraged, and wouldn't venture further. So he climbed out again on to the

side nearer to his own house, and told me I could possess
the brave new country alone. He went his way, and I came
mine; he followed Obstinate and I came to this gate.'

*A man may have company when he sets out for heaven, and
yet enter alone*

Then Goodwill said, 'Poor fellow, does heavenly splendour
mean so little to him that he thinks it's not worth risking a
few difficulties to obtain it?'

Christian accuses himself before the man at the gate

Christian said, 'I've told the truth about Pliable, but if I
should also tell all the truth about myself it would seem as
though I'm no better than he. True, Pliable went back to his
own house, but I also turned aside to tread the way of
death, after being persuaded by the worldly arguments of a
man called Mr Worldly-Wiseman.'

'Oh! Did he come across you? Did he want you to seek
relief at the hands of Mr Legality? They're both of them
downright cheats. And did you take his advice?

'Yes, as far as I dared. I went to find Mr Legality until I
thought the mountain by his house would fall on my head.
Then I was forced to stop.'

'That mountain has been the death of many, and will be
the death of many more. It's a good thing you escaped
being dashed to pieces by it.'

'Honestly, I've no idea what would have become of me
there if Evangelist had not met me again. He found me
when I was down in the dumps and wondering what to do.
It was by God's mercy that he came to me, otherwise I'd
never have come here. But now here I am, such as I am,
more fit for death by that mountain, than to stand like this
talking with you, my lord. What a kindness this is! Despite

everything I'm still admitted here!'

Goodwill said, 'We raise no objections against anyone. It doesn't matter what they've done before coming here, they'll never be driven away (John 6:37). So, my dear Christian, come a little way with me, and I'll teach you about the way you must travel. Look ahead. Do you see this narrow path? That's the way you must go. It was marked out by the patriarchs and prophets, by Christ and his apostles, and it is as straight as a rule can make it. This is the way you must walk.'

Christian is afraid of losing his way

'But,' Christian said, 'are there no turnings or bends which could make a stranger lose his way?'

'Yes, many paths lead off into another road lower than this, but they're crooked and wide. You can distinguish the right way from the wrong, because only the right way is straight and narrow' (Matt. 7:14).

Christian is weary of his burden

Then in my dream I saw that Christian asked Goodwill if he could help him take off the burden that was on his back, because he'd still not got rid of it, nor could he without help.

Goodwill said to Christian, 'Be content to bear your burden until you come to the place of deliverance. There it will fall from your back by itself.'

Christian then began to get ready for his journey and Goodwill told him that when he had gone some distance from the gate, he would come to the house of the Interpreter. He said that Christian should knock at his door and the Interpreter would show him some excellent things. Then Christian took leave of his friend, who again bid him Godspeed.

5

The Interpreter's House

Christian went on until he came to the Interpreter's house. He knocked over and over again until at last someone came to the door and asked who was there.

Christian said, 'Sir, I'm a traveller, and I've been told by an acquaintance of the owner of this house that it would be good for me to call here. I'd therefore like to speak with the master of the house.'

So the servant called for the master of the house who, after a little while, came to Christian and asked him what he wanted.

'Sir,' said Christian, 'I've come from the City of Destruction and am travelling to Mount Zion. I was told by the man who stands at the gate at the top of this road that if I called here you would show me some excellent things, things that would help me on my journey.'

Christian is shown a picture

Then the Interpreter said, 'Come in. What I'll show you will do you good.'

He commanded his servant to light a candle and told Christian to follow him. First he took Christian into a private room and told his servant to open a door. When he had done this Christian saw a picture of a person of very great importance hanging against the wall. This was what it looked like: the man's eyes were lifted up to heaven; he held the best of books in his hands; the law of truth was written on his lips; and the world was behind his back. He stood as if he pleaded with men, and a crown of gold hung over his head.

Then Christian said, 'What does it mean?'

The meaning of the picture

The Interpreter explained: 'The man whose picture this is, is one in a million. He can become a father (1 Cor. 4:15), endure the pains of childbirth (Gal. 4:19) and be like a mother caring for her little children when they are born (1 Thess. 2:7). His eyes are lifted up to heaven, the best of books is in his hands, and the law of truth is written on his lips, to show you that his work is to know and unfold dark things to sinners. He is standing as if he pleaded with men, with the world cast behind him, and a crown over his head, to show that he slights and despises the things of the present for the love he has for his master's service, and therefore he is sure to possess glory as his reward in the world to come.'

Why the Interpreter showed Christian the picture first of all

'Now,' said the Interpreter, 'I've shown you this picture first because this is a picture of the man, the only man, whom the lord of the place you travel to has authorised to be your guide in whatever difficulties you encounter on the way. So make careful note of what I have shown you, and keep it firmly in mind, lest in your travels you meet with some who pretend to lead you aright, but whose way goes down to death.'

Then the Interpreter took Christian by the hand, and led him into a very large parlour. It was full of dust, because it was never swept. After he had looked at it a little while, the Interpreter called for a man to sweep it. When he began to sweep, thick dust flew up so that Christian was almost choked. Then the Interpreter called a maid standing by. 'Bring some water and sprinkle the room,' he said. When she had done this, it was swept and cleaned with no trouble.

Christian asked, 'What does this mean?'

The Interpreter answered, 'This parlour is the heart of a man who has never been sanctified by the sweet grace of the gospel. The dust is his original sin and inward corruption which have defiled his whole personality. The one who began to sweep at first is the law; but the one who brought water, and sprinkled it, is the gospel. You saw how, as soon as the first man began to sweep, the dust flew about so much that it was impossible to clean the room. You were almost choked instead. This is to show you that the law, instead of cleansing the heart from sin, makes sin spring into life. The law gives strength to sin, and then goes on to increase sin's strength within the soul, even as it reveals and forbids it, because it doesn't have the power to subdue it (Rom. 5:20; 7:9; 1 Cor. 15:56).

'Again, you saw the maid lay the dust by sprinkling the floor, and then contentedly clean the room, to show you that when the gospel comes into the heart with its sweet and precious power then sin is vanquished and subdued. The soul is made clean through its faith and fit for the king of glory to inhabit' (John 15:3; Acts 15:9; Rom. 16:25–6; Eph. 5:26).

The Interpreter shows Christian Passion and Patience

Then in my dream I saw that the Interpreter took Christian by the hand and led him to a little room where two small children each sat in his own chair. The name of the elder was Passion, and the younger, Patience. Passion seemed to be very discontented, but Patience was quiet.

Then Christian asked, 'Why is Passion so cross?'

The Interpreter answered, 'Their master wants Passion

to wait for the best things until the beginning of next year, but he wants it all now. Patience is willing to wait.'

Then I saw someone come to Passion with a bag of treasure and pour it at his feet. Passion eagerly picked it all up and laughed Patience to scorn. But I saw that very soon Passion had squandered the lot and had nothing left but his rags.

Then Christian said to the Interpreter, 'Explain this more fully to me.'

So the Interpreter said, 'These two lads are types. Passion stands for the people of this world, and Patience for the people of the world to come. As you can see, Passion wants to have everything now, this year, that is to say, in this world. The people of this world are like that. They must have all their good things now, they can't wait till next year, that is, until the next world, for their share. That proverb, "A bird in the hand is worth two in the bush", carries more weight with them than all the divine promises of good in the world to come. But as you saw, Passion quickly squandered everything, and was soon left with nothing but rags. That's how it will be with all such people at the end of this world.'

Then Christian said, 'Now I see that Patience is wiser, and for a number of reasons. First, because he waits for the best things and second because he will still possess his glory when the other has nothing but rags.'

'And you may add another,' said the Interpreter. 'The glory of the next world will never wear out, whereas these things are suddenly gone. So Passion doesn't have much reason to laugh at Patience because he had his good things first. Patience will have more reason to laugh at Passion, because he had his best things last. For *first* must give place to *last*; *last* still has his time to come and gives place to nothing, for there is no one else to succeed. He, then, who has his share *first* must spend it over the course of time; but he that has his share *last* will have it for all time. So it's said of Dives, "In your lifetime you received your good things, while Lazarus received bad things, but now he is comforted here"' (Luke 16:25).

'I can see it's not best to covet things that belong to now, but to wait for the things to come,' said Christian.

'What you say is the truth: "For what is seen is temporary, but what is unseen is eternal" (2 Cor. 4:18). But, though this is true, yet, because things in the present and our bodily appetites are so closely related one to another, and because things to come and our worldly feelings are such strangers to one another, the first of these pairs suddenly fall into friendship, and the second are far apart.'

The Interpreter shows Christian a fire

Then in my dream I saw the Interpreter take Christian by the hand and lead him into a place where there was a fire burning against a wall, and someone standing by, throwing a great deal of water on it to put it out. But the fire kept burning higher and hotter.

Then Christian said, 'What's the meaning of this?'

The Interpreter answered, 'This fire is the work of grace in the heart. The one who throws water on it to extinguish it is the devil. But, as you can see, in spite of that the fire burns higher and hotter. I'll show you the reason for that.'

He took him behind the wall where he saw a man holding a container of oil, out of which he continually and secretly threw oil into the fire.

Then Christian said, 'What does this mean?'

The Interpreter answered, 'This is Christ. With the oil of his grace he continually maintains the work already begun in the heart. In this way, no matter what the devil can do, the souls of Christ's people remain full of grace (2 Cor. 12:9). And you saw the man standing behind the wall to keep the fire going to teach you that it's hard for people being tempted to see how this work of grace is maintained in the soul.'

Once again the Interpreter took Christian by the hand. He led him into a pleasant place where a magnificent palace, beautiful to look at, had been built and Christian was delighted with the sight. On the top of it he saw people walking who were clothed all in gold.

The valiant man

Then Christian asked, 'May we go there?'

The Interpreter took him and led him up towards the door of the palace. And what a sight! At the door a huge gathering of people waited to go in, longing, but not daring to enter. A little away from the door a man sat at a table with a book and inkhorn in front of him. He was taking the names of the people who could enter the palace. Christian saw that many men in armour were standing on guard outside the doorway, resolved to do what damage and harm they could to whoever wanted to enter. This quite amazed Christian. Everyone began to move back for fear of the armed men, but at last Christian saw a man with a very determined expression on his face come up to the man who sat there writing.

'Set down my name, sir,' he said. This accomplished, the man drew his sword and put on his helmet. He then rushed at the door and the armed men, who retaliated with deadly force. But the man, not at all discouraged, fell to cutting and hacking most fiercely. After receiving and inflicting many wounds he cut his way through all his opponents, and pressed forward to the palace (Acts 14:22). At this a pleasant voice could be heard by those who were inside, and even by those who walked on the top of the palace. It said,

> Come in, come in;
> Eternal glory thou shalt win.

So the strong man went in, and was given clothes to wear like those within the palace. Then Christian smiled. 'I really think I know the meaning of this,' he said.

Despair in an iron cage

'Now,' said Christian, 'let me go there.'

'No,' said the Interpreter, 'wait till I have shown you a little more, and after that you can go on your way.'

So he took him by the hand again, and led him into a very dark room, where a man sat in an iron cage.

Now the man seemed very sad: he sat looking down to the ground, his hands clasped together, and he sighed as if his heart would break.

'What does this mean?' asked Christian.

The Interpreter told him to talk with the man.

So Christian said, 'Who are you?'

The man answered, 'I am who I was not once.'

'Who were you once?' asked Christian.

'I was once a good believer. Both in my own eyes and in the eyes of others I was growing in the faith. Once I thought I was set for the Celestial City, and had a quiet confidence and joy that I'd get there' (Luke 8:13).

'Well, who are you now?

'Now I'm a man of despair, shut up in despair, as I'm shut up in this iron cage. I can't get out; oh, *now* I can't.'

'But how did you come to be in this condition?'

'I left off being alert and self-controlled. I dropped the reins on the neck of my lusts. I sinned against the light of the word, and the goodness of God. I've grieved the Spirit, and he's gone. I tempted the devil, and he's come to me; I've provoked God to anger, and he's left me. I've hardened my heart till I *cannot* repent.'

Then Christian said to the Interpreter, 'But is there no hope for such a man as this?'

'Ask him,' said the Interpreter.

So Christian asked, 'Is there no hope? Must you be kept in this iron cage of despair?'

'No, none at all,' said the man.

'Why? The Son of the Blessed is full of pity.'

'I've crucified the Son of God all over again (Heb. 6:6).

I've despised his person (Luke 19:14). I've despised his righteousness. I've treated his blood as an unholy thing. I've insulted the Spirit of grace (Heb. 10:26–9). So I have shut myself out of all the promises, and now there remains nothing but threatenings, dreadful threatenings, fearful threatenings of certain judgment and fiery fury, which shall devour me like an enemy.'

'Why did you bring yourself into this condition?' Christian asked.

'For the passions, pleasures, and advantages of this world. In these enjoyments I promised myself considerable delight. But now every one of those things bites me and gnaws at me like a burning worm.'

'But can't you repent and turn?'

'God has denied me repentance. His word gives me no encouragement to believe. Indeed, he himself has shut me up in this iron cage and all the men in the world cannot let me out. Oh eternity! Eternity! How shall I grapple with the misery that I must meet in eternity!'

Then the Interpreter said to Christian, 'Remember this man's misery. Let it be an everlasting warning to you.'

'Well,' said Christian, 'this is fearful! God help me to be alert and self-controlled, and to pray that I may shun the cause of this man's misery. Sir, isn't it time for me to go on my way now?'

'Wait till I've shown you one more thing, and then you can go on your way.'

So the Interpreter took Christian by the hand again, and led him into a room where a man was getting out of bed. As he put on his clothes he shook and trembled.

'Why does he tremble like this?' asked Christian.

The Interpreter then asked the man to tell Christian the reason. So he began, 'Last night, as I was asleep, I dreamed. Before my eyes the heavens grew immensely black. It thundered and lightning struck in a terrifying way, which sent me into an agony. As I looked up in my dream I saw the clouds race by at an unusual pace. And then I heard a great trumpet call, and saw a man sitting on a cloud, attended by thousands of the heavenly host. They were all in flaming fire and the heavens themselves were a burning flame.

'Then I heard a voice, saying, "Arise, you dead, and come to judgment"; and with that the rocks split, the graves opened, and the dead came out (1 Cor. 15; 1 Thess. 4; Jude v.15; 2 Thess. 1:7; Rev. 20:11–14). Some of them were extremely glad and looked upwards; some sought to hide themselves under the mountains. Then I saw the man who sat upon the cloud open the book and bid the world draw near (Ps. 1:1–3; Isa. 26:21; Mic. 7:16–17). Yet, because of a fierce flame that sprang up in front of him, a suitable distance lay between the judge and the prisoners at the bar (Dan. 7:9–10; Mal.3:2–3).

'And I also heard it proclaimed to those who attended the man seated on the cloud, "Gather together the weeds, chaff, and stubble, and cast them into the burning lake" (Matt. 3:12; 13:30; Mal. 4:1). And with that the bottomless pit opened just where I was standing. Out of its mouth billowed smoke, and coals of fire, with hideous noises. And those same attendants were told, "Gather the wheat into the barn" (Luke 3:17). After that I saw many people caught up together and carried away into the clouds (1 Thess. 4:16–17); but I was left behind. I too sought to hide, but I could not, for the man who sat upon the cloud still kept his eye upon me. My sins came to mind, and my conscience accused me on every side (Rom. 2:14–15). And then I woke up from my sleep.'

'But what was it that made you so afraid of this sight?' asked Christian.

'Why, I thought that the day of judgment had come, and that I wasn't ready for it. But what frightened me most was that the angels gathered up some people, and left me behind. Also the pit of hell opened her mouth just where I was standing. My conscience, too, accused me and it seemed that the judge didn't take his eyes off me, and his face was full of wrath.'

Then the Interpreter asked Christian, 'Have you considered all these things?'

'Yes,' said Christian, 'and they fill me with hope and fear.'

'Well, keep all these things in your mind so that they may be a spur in your side to urge you forward in the way you must go.' So Christian began to get ready for his journey.

Then the Interpreter said, 'May the Comforter always be with you, dear Christian, to guide you in the way that leads to the city.'

So Christian went on his way, saying,

> Here I have seen things rare and profitable;
> Things pleasant, dreadful, things to make me stable
> In what I have begun to take in hand:
> Then let me think on them, and understand
> Wherefore they shew'd me were; and let me be
> Thankful, O good Interpreter, to thee.

6

The Cross and the Contrast

Now in my dream I saw that the highway along which Christian was to travel was closed in on either side by a wall, and that wall was called Salvation (Isa. 26:1). So up this way burdened Christian ran, but not without great difficulty because of the load on his back.

He ran till he came to a slight upward slope, on the top of which stood a cross. A little below it, at the bottom, was a tomb. I saw in my dream that just as Christian came up to the cross his burden came loose from his shoulders, and fell off his back. It began to tumble down hill, and continued rolling till it came to the mouth of the tomb, where it fell in, and I saw it no more.

How glad and lighthearted Christian was! With a happy heart he said, 'He has given me rest by his sorrow, and life by his death.' Then he stood still for a while to look and wonder. He found it very surprising that the sight of the cross should ease him of his burden like this. He gazed and gazed till the springs in his head sent tears down his cheeks (Zech. 12:10).

Now as he stood looking and weeping three Shining Ones approached him. They greeted him with the words, 'Peace be to you.' The first said to him, 'Your sins are forgiven' (Mark 2:5); the second stripped him of his rags, and dressed him in a fresh set of clothes. The third set a mark on his forehead, and gave him a scroll with a seal on it (Zech. 3:4; Eph. 1:13). He told him to look at this as he ran, and to hand it in at the Celestial Gate. Then they went on their way.

Christian gave three leaps for joy, and went off singing:

> Thus far did I come laden with my sin,
> Nor could ought ease the grief that I was in,
> Till I came hither; what a place is this!
> Must here be the beginning of my bliss?
> Must here the burden fall from off my back?
> Must here the strings that bound it to me crack?
> Blest cross! Blest sepulchre! Blest rather be
> The Man that there was put to shame for me!

I saw Christian continue until he came to the bottom of the slope, where, a little way from the path, he saw three men with fetters on their heels lying fast asleep. One was called Simple, another Sloth and the third Presumption.

Christian, seeing them asleep like that, went up to them, hoping he might wake them. He cried, 'You are like someone sleeping on the high seas, lying on top of the rigging' (Prov. 23:34). 'Wake up, and come away; if you want I'll help you get your fetters off.' He continued, 'If he that prowls around like a roaring lion is looking for someone to devour, you will certainly become a prey to his teeth' (1 Pet. 5:8).

At that they looked up at him, and began to reply like this:
Simple said, 'I can't see any danger.'
Sloth said, 'Oh, just a little more sleep.'
And Presumption said, 'Every barrel must stand on its own bottom.'

So they lay down and went to sleep again, and Christian went on his way. But it upset him to think that men in such danger should think so little of his kindness in freely offering to help them by waking them, advising them, and helping to take off their irons. And as he was troubled by this, he caught sight of two men who came tumbling over the wall on the left-hand side of the narrow way, and he hurried to catch them up. One was named Formalist, and the other Hypocrisy. As he drew near, Christian entered into conversation with them.

'Gentlemen,' Christian said, 'where've you come from and where are you off to?'

'We were born in the land of Vain-glory, and are going for praise to Mount Zion,' they replied.

'Why didn't you come in at the gate which stands at the beginning of the path?' asked Christian. 'Don't you know that it's written, "The man who does not enter the sheep pen by the gate, but climbs in by some other way, is a thief and a robber"?' (John 10:1).

They replied that all their countrymen considered it much too far to go all the way to the gate to enter, and their usual way was to take a short cut. So everyone climbed over the wall, as they had just done.

'But won't it be regarded as an offence against the Lord of the city to which we are bound, to violate his clear rules in this way?' asked Christian.

Formalist and Hypocrisy replied that Christian need not trouble his head about those things because it was traditional to do this. They said that if need be they could produce testimony bearing witness to it, which went back over a thousand years.

'But,' Christian said, 'will your practice stand a trial at law?'

They told him that without any doubt tradition that had lasted more than a thousand years would now be admitted as legal practice by any impartial judge. And besides, they said, as long as they got on to the path what did it matter which way they got in?

'If we're in, we're in,' they said. 'You're on the path, as we can see, by entering in at the gate. We're also on the path by clambering over the wall. How, then, are you better off than we?'

Christian replied, 'I'm walking by the rule of my master; you're following the ignorant devices of your own whims. You're regarded as thieves already by the Lord of the way. So I doubt that the end of the way will find you true. You came in by yourselves without his direction, and shall go out by yourselves without his mercy.'

To this they gave little response, except to tell him to look out for himself. Then I saw that they all went on, every man in his way, without much exchange between them, apart from when the two men told Christian that as far as laws and ordinances were concerned, they had no doubt that they would be as conscientious as he.

'So,' they said, 'we see no difference between us, except the coat you're wearing which was, we suspect, given you by some of your neighbours to hide the shame of your nakedness.'

Christian replied, 'You didn't come in by the door, but a man is not justified by observing the law (Gal. 2:16). And as for this coat, it was given me by the Lord of the place I'm going to, in order, as you say, to cover my nakedness. I take it as a token of his kindness to me, for I had nothing but rags before. Besides, it's what comforts me on my journey. Surely, I think, when I come to the gate of the city its Lord will think well of me, since I have his coat on my back. He freely gave me this coat on the day he stripped me of my rags. Moreover, I've a mark on my forehead which you've perhaps not noticed. One of my Lord's closest friends fixed it there the day my burden fell off my shoulders. What's more, a sealed scroll was given me to comfort me on the way. I was also told to give it in at the Celestial Gate, as a token of my certain entry. I doubt you have any of these things – you missed them because you didn't enter in at the gate.'

They said nothing to all this, but only looked at each other and laughed. Then I saw them all continue their journey, only Christian kept ahead and had no more to say to anyone but himself. That he sometimes did sorrowfully and sometimes cheerfully. He also often read from the roll that one of the Shining Ones had given him, and this refreshed him.

7

The Hill Difficulty

I saw then that they arrived at the foot of the Hill Difficulty where there was a spring. Two other paths led off from this spring, as well as the one which came straight from the gate; one of these paths turned to the left, and the other to the right, round the bottom of the hill. But the narrow way lay right up the hillside. Because of the climb up the side of the hill it is called Difficulty. Christian went to the spring and drank to refresh himself (Isa. 49:10). He then began to climb up the hill, saying to himself:

> This hill, though high, I covet to ascend;
> The difficulty will not me offend,
> For I perceive the way to life lies here.
> Come, pluck up, heart, let's neither faint nor fear:
> Better, though difficult, the right way to go,
> Than wrong, though easy, where the end is woe.

The other two men also came to the foot of the hill, but when they saw how steep and high the hill was, and that there were two other paths, they supposed that these two ways would meet up again with Christian's path on the other side of the hill and resolved to travel along those paths. (Now the name of one was Danger, and the other Destruction.) So one took Danger Road, which led him into a great wood. The other went directly up the path to Destruction, which led him into a wide field from which rose dark mountains. There he stumbled and fell, and didn't rise again.

I looked for Christian and saw him going up the hill, where he slowed from running to walking, and from walking to clambering on his hands and knees because the slope was so steep. Now about half-way up there was a pleasant arbour, made by the Lord of the hill, where tired travellers could refresh themselves. There Christian sat down to rest. Pulling his scroll from his breast, he read to his great comfort. He also began to examine the coat or garment that had been given him when he had been standing by the cross. And so, enjoying himself in this way, he at last fell into a deep sleep, which was to detain him in that place until it was almost night. And as he slept his scroll fell out of his hand. Then a man came to him and woke him up, saying, 'Go to the ant, you sluggard; consider its ways and be wise!' (Prov. 6:6). With that Christian suddenly sat up, and hurried on his way. He climbed quickly till he came to the top of the hill.

When he reached the top of the hill, two men came running at full speed towards him. The name of one was Timorous, and the other Mistrust. Christian said to them, 'Sirs, what's the matter? You're running the wrong way.'

Timorous answered that they had been going to the City of Zion, and had got past Christian's difficult place. 'But,' he continued, 'the farther we go, the more danger we meet with, so we've turned, and are going back again.'

'Yes,' said Mistrust, 'for on the path just ahead lie a couple of lions. We'd no idea whether they were asleep or not, all we could think was that if we came within reach, they'd pull us to pieces.'

Christian loses his scroll

Then Christian said, 'You're making me feel afraid. But where shall I fly to be safe? I can't go back to my own country, it's ripe for fire and sulphur and I shall certainly die there. But if I can get to the Celestial City, I'm sure to be safe. I must venture on. To go back is nothing but sure death; to go forward brings the fear of death, and life everlasting beyond it. I'll still go forward.'

So Mistrust and Timorous ran down the hill and Christian went on his way. But thinking again of what he had heard from the men, he felt against his breast for his scroll, so that he might read it and be encouraged. But it wasn't there. Christian was in great distress. He didn't know what to do. He wanted what used to bring relief to him, and should have been his pass into the Celestial City. He was very puzzled and didn't know what to do. At last he remembered that he had slept in the arbour on the side of the hill and falling down on his knees he asked God's forgiveness for that foolish act. Then he went back. Who can adequately describe the sorrow in Christian's heart? Sometimes he sighed, sometimes he wept. Often he was angry with himself for being foolish enough to fall asleep in a place which had been built only to provide a little refreshment for weary travellers. In this state he returned, carefully looking to one side and then the other as he went in the hope that he might find this scroll which had been his comfort so many times on his journey.

He continued on like this till he came again within sight of the arbour where he had sat and slept. But the sight of it brought a fresh surge of sorrow as he remembered all over again the evil of his sleeping.

So he kept bewailing his sinful sleep, saying, 'Oh, wretched man that I am! How could I sleep in the daytime! How could I sleep in the midst of difficulty! (1 Thess. 5:7–8; Rev. 2:4–5) How could I indulge the flesh by using that arbour to satisfy my physical needs when the Lord of the hill had erected it only for the relief of the spirits of pilgrims! How many steps have I taken in vain! This is what happened to Israel; for their sin they were sent back again by the way of the Red Sea. I am forced to tread with sorrow, when I might have walked with delight if only it had not been for this sinful sleep. How far I might have travelled on my way by this time! Now I have to tread this path three times when I need only have walked it once. Yes, and now I'm likely to be caught by the night since the day is almost over. Oh, how I wish I'd not slept!'

Christian finds his scroll where he lost it

Now by this time Christian had come to the arbour again. There, for a while, he sat down and wept. But at last (as Christian would have it) looking sorrowfully down under the bench, there he spotted his scroll! Trembling all over he hastily picked it up and put it against his breast. Who can describe how joyful this man was when he had retrieved his roll which assured him of his life and guaranteed acceptance at the desired heaven! So he placed it against his breast, gave thanks to God for directing his eye to the spot where it lay, and with joy and tears set off again on his journey. How nimbly he ran up the rest of the hill! Yet before he gained the summit, the sun went down upon Christian. This made him once more recall the stupidity of his sleeping and he was again full of grief.

'Oh, sinful sleep!' he said. 'Because of you I'm caught by the dark. I must walk without the sun, darkness will cover the path at my feet, and I will hear the noise of mournful creatures, all because of my sinful sleep!'

Christian is fearful of the lions

Now Christian remembered how Mistrust and Timorous had told him that they were frightened by the sight of the lions. He spoke to himself again: 'These beasts range in the night for their prey, and if they meet me in the dark how will I elude them? How can I escape being torn in pieces by them?'

And so he journeyed on. But while he was bewailing his plight he raised his eyes and saw there in front of him a great palace. It was called Beautiful, and it stood just by the side of the road.

8

The Palace Beautiful

In my dream I saw Christian rush forward, in the hope that he might stay there. Before he had gone far he entered a very narrow passage, about two hundred metres from the porter's lodge, and watching very carefully as he went, he saw two lions on the path.

Now I can see the dangers that drove Mistrust and Timorous back, Christian thought. He didn't notice that the lions were chained, and he was afraid. He considered going back himself for he thought that nothing but death lay ahead. But the porter at the lodge, whose name was Watchful, saw Christian stop as if to go back and cried out to him, 'Is your strength so small (Mark 4:40)? Don't be afraid of the lions, they're chained. They're placed there to test faith where it exists, and to find out those who have none. Keep to the middle of the path and no harm will come to you.'

Then I saw him go on, trembling with fear because of the lions, and paying careful attention to the porter's directions. Christian heard the lions roar, but they didn't harm him. He clapped his hands and went on, till at last he stood before the porter at the gate.

Then Christian said to the porter, 'Sir, what is this house, and may I stay here tonight?'

The porter answered, 'This house was built by the Lord of the hill for the refreshment and safety of pilgrims.' The porter also asked where Christian was from and where he was going.

Christian said, 'I'm from the City of Destruction, and I'm

going to Mount Zion. But because it's dark now I'd like, if I may, to stay here tonight.'

'What's your name?' asked the porter.

'My name is now Christian. But originally my name was Graceless. I come from the race of Japheth whom God will persuade to dwell in the tents of Shem' (Gen. 9:27).

'But why have you arrived so late? The sun's gone down.'

'I'd have been here sooner, but wretch that I am I slept in the arbour on the hillside. Even so, I'd have been here much sooner, but then in my sleep I lost my evidence and came without it to the brow of the hill. Then, feeling for it I couldn't find it. In great sorrow I was forced to go back to the place where I'd slept and there I found it again; and now I'm here.'

'Well, I'll call one of the young ladies of this place. In accordance with the rules of the house, if she likes what you have to say she'll take you in to the rest of the family.'

So Watchful the porter rang a bell, and the sound of it brought a dignified and beautiful young lady named Discretion to the door. Discretion wanted to know why she had been called.

The porter answered, 'This man is on a journey from the City of Destruction to Mount Zion. He's tired and has been overtaken by the night, so he's asked me if he can stay here tonight. I told him I'd call you and said you'd decide what was the right thing to do after you'd talked with him, as is the rule of the house.'

So Discretion asked Christian all about himself: where he was from and where and how he'd got on to the path. She also asked him what he'd seen and whom he'd met on the way, and Christian told her. Finally she asked his name.

'It's Christian,' he said, 'and I want to stay here tonight, all the more because, from what I see, this place was built by the Lord of the hill for the refreshment and safety of pilgrims.'

Prudence, Piety and Charity

So she smiled, but tears formed in her eyes. After a short pause she said, 'I'll call two or three more of the family.' She ran to the door, and called out Prudence, Piety, and Charity, who, after a little more conversation with Christian, drew him into the family.

Many of them met him at the threshold of the house and said, 'Come in, you're blessed by the Lord. This house was built by the Lord of the hill for the purpose of taking care of pilgrims like yourself.'

Christian nodded, and followed them into the house. When he was sitting down they gave him something to drink, and agreed that they should make the most of the time until supper was ready by getting some of their number to talk with Christian. They selected Piety, Prudence and Charity to talk with Christian and the conversation went as follows.

'Well, dear Christian,' began Piety. 'now we have so lovingly received you into our house tonight, let's see if we ourselves can gain from it by talking with you about all the things that have happened to you in your pilgrimage.'

'I'll be delighted to talk with you,' said Christian. 'And I'm glad this is what you want.'

'What first moved you to take to a pilgrim's life?' asked Piety.

Christian said, 'I was driven out of my own country by a dreadful sound in my ears, telling me that unavoidable destruction would befall me if I stayed there.'

'But what made you come this way?'

How Christian got on to the path to Zion

'It was God's will. When I was under the threat of destruction, I didn't know which way to go, but as chance would have it a man came to me as I was trembling and weeping. His name was Evangelist and he directed me to the wicket-gate, which I'd never have found by myself. And so he put me on to the path that has led me straight to this house.'

'But didn't you pass by the Interpreter's house?' asked Piety.

'Yes, and saw such sights there, things that I'll remember and that will stick with me as long as I live. Three things especially: how Christ, despite Satan, maintains his work of grace in the heart; the man who sinned himself right out of the hope of God's mercy; and also the dream of the man who thought in his sleep that the Day of Judgment had come.'

'Why? Did you hear him tell his dream?'

'Yes, and I thought it was dreadful. It made my heart ache as he was telling me, yet I'm glad I heard it.'

'Was that all you saw at the Interpreter's house?'

'No. He led me to where there was a magnificent palace whose inhabitants were clothed in gold. I saw how one courageous man cut his way through the armed guard that stood at the door to keep him out; and how he was welcomed in and given eternal glory. Those things thrilled my heart. I could have stayed at that good man's house for a year, but I knew I still had far to go.'

'And what else did you see on the way?' asked Piety.

'See! Why a little farther on I saw Someone who, it seemed to me, was hanging bleeding on the tree. The very sight of him made my burden fall off my back! (You see, I'd been groaning under a weary burden.) But then it just fell off. It was strange. I'd never seen anything like it before. In fact, while I stood looking – because I could not stop gazing on him – Three Shining Ones came to me. One of them witnessed to the fact that my sins were forgiven; another stripped me of my rags and gave me this embroidered coat which you see; and the third set this mark on my forehead, and gave me this sealed scroll.' With that Christian pulled it out.

'But you saw more than this, didn't you?' Piety said.

'I've told you the best things, but I saw some other smaller things. For instance, I saw three men, Simple, Sloth, and Presumption, fast asleep just off the path, and their heels were chained in irons. But do you think I could wake them up! I also saw Formalist and Hypocrisy clambering over the wall, to go, as they seemed to think, to Zion, but they very quickly got lost. I told them they would, but they wouldn't believe me. But chiefly I found it hard work to get up this hill. And just as hard to pass by the lions' mouths. Honestly, if it hadn't been for that good man, the porter, who stands at the gate, I'm not sure, after all, that I might not have gone back again. But now I thank God I'm here, and I thank you for taking me in.'

Prudence talks with Christian

Then Prudence thought it would be good to ask Christian a few questions and hear his answers.

'Don't you sometimes think of the country you've left?' Prudence said.

'Yes, but with great shame and dislike. If I'd been regretting the country I'd left I'd have had opportunities to return. But now I long for a better country – a heavenly one' (Heb. 11:15–16).

'Didn't you bring any of the things that you were once familiar with?'

'Yes, but very much against my will, especially my worldly thoughts which I used to delight in, as did all my fellow countrymen. But now all those things bring me sorrow and if it were up to me I'd choose never to think of them again. Yet when I want to do the best, the worst is with me' (Rom. 7:14–23).

'Don't you sometimes find that those things which trouble you can be overcome?'

How Christian gets power against his corruptions

Christian told Prudence, 'Yes, but that seldom happens.

They're golden hours when it does.'

'Can you remember how your troubles are sometimes overcome?' Prudence continued.

'Yes, when I think about what I saw at the cross. That does it. And when I look at my embroidered coat, that will do it. Also when I look into the scroll that I'm carrying, that helps, too. And when I think longingly about the place I'm travelling to, then that will also do it.'

'And what is it that makes you so want to go to Mount Zion?'

'Why, there I hope to see the one alive who once hung dead on the cross. There I hope to be rid of all those things which to this day still trouble me. There they say there is no death (Isa. 25:8; Rev. 21:4), and there I shall dwell with the kind of friends I like best. To tell you the truth, I love him, because he freed me of my burden, and I'm weary of my inward sickness. I long to be where I'll die no more, and with people who'll cry out continually, "Holy, holy, holy".'

Charity talks with Christian

Then Charity spoke to Christian. 'Have you a family? Are you a married man?' she asked.

'I have a wife and four small children.'

'And why didn't you bring them along with you?'

Then Christian wept. 'How willingly I would have done! But they were all utterly averse to my going on this pilgrimage.'

'But you should have talked to them. You should have tried to show them the danger of being left behind.'

'I did. And I told them what God had showed me about the destruction of our city; but they thought I was joking and wouldn't believe me.' (Gen. 19:14).

'And did you pray to God to bless your advice to them?' asked Charity.

'Yes, and with great love in my heart, because you must

know that my wife and poor children were very dear to me.'

'But did you tell them about your own sorrow, and fear of destruction? For I suppose that the destruction was clear enough to you?'

'Yes, over and over again. And they also saw my fear in my face, and in my tears, and in the way I trembled at the thought of the judgment that hung over our heads. But nothing could persuade them to come with me.'

'But how did they explain their refusal to join you?'

'Well, my wife was afraid of losing this world, and my children were given over to the foolish delights of youth. So what with one thing and another they left me to go off by myself like this.'

'But didn't your empty life throw a damper on all that your persuasive words might have achieved?'

'Certainly I cannot commend my life. I'm conscious of my many failings. I also know that a man's behaviour can undo everything that, with all his arguments and powers of persuasion, he's struggled to instil into others for their good. Yet, this I can say: I was very careful lest any wrong action of mine should put them off joining me on this pilgrimage. In fact, because of this they told me I was too strict and denied myself things in which they saw no evil – and I'd done this for their sakes! No, I think I can say that if anything in me did put them off, it was my great fear of sinning against God, or of doing anything wrong to my neighbour.'

'Yes, Cain hated his brother because his own actions were evil and his brother's were righteous (1 John 3:12), and if your wife and children have taken offence because of this it indicates that they are hardened against good, and you won't be held accountable for their blood' (Ezek. 3:19).

Now in my dream I saw that they sat talking together like this until supper was prepared. When they were ready they sat down to eat. The table was laid with rich food and fine wine, and all their talk at the table was about the Lord of the hill. They spoke about what he had done, and why he had done it and why he had built that house. From what they said I could see that he had been a great warrior, and had fought with and killed the one that had the power of death (Heb. 2:14–15), but not without great danger to himself, which made me love him all the more.

'For, as I believe, and as you say,' added Christian, 'he did it with the loss of a great deal of blood. But what put the glory of grace into all he did was that he did it out of pure love for his country.'

Others from the household said that they had seen and spoken with him since he died on the cross. And they testified that they had heard from his own lips of his great love for poor pilgrims, so that there is no one like him from the east to the west.

Christ makes princes out of beggars

Furthermore, they gave as an example of this that he had stripped himself of his glory for the poor. They heard him affirm that he wouldn't dwell on the Mountain of Zion alone. Moreover, they said that he had given many pilgrims the honour of being princes, though they had been born beggars, and had come from the ash heap (1 Sam. 2:8).

So they talked together till late into the night, and then after they had committed themselves to their Lord for protection, they went to bed. They put Christian in a large upper room, called Peace, the window of which opened towards the rising sun. There he slept till daybreak. When he awoke, he sang,

> Where am I now? Is this the love and care
> Of Jesus, for the men that pilgrims are?
> Thus to provide! That I should be forgiven!
> And dwell already the next door to heaven.

Christian goes into the study, and what he sees there

In the morning they got up and talked again. They told him
not to go till they had showed him the rare possessions of that
place. First they took him into the study where they showed
him records of the greatest antiquity. As I remember my
dream, these records showed the genealogy of the Lord of
the hill: he was the Son of the Ancient of Days, and had
been born of an eternal generation. Here also there was
more information about the deeds that he had done, and
the names of many hundreds of people whom he had taken
into his service and placed in dwelling-places that neither
time nor natural decay could ever destroy.

Then they read to Christian some of the noble acts per-
formed by some of the Lord's servants, how they had
'through faith conquered kingdoms, administered justice,
and gained what was promised; who shut the mouths of
lions, quenched the fury of the flames, and escaped the
edge of the sword; whose weakness was turned into
strength; and who became powerful in battle and routed
foreign armies' (Heb. 11:33–4).

Then again, in another part of the records, they read how
willing their Lord was to receive anyone into his service. He
would accept everyone, even someone who in times past
had openly insulted his person and work. There were also
several other historical records of many famous things, all
of which Christian looked at. There were things both
ancient and modern, together with prophecies and predic-
tions of things that will certainly be fulfilled, to the dread
and amazement of his enemies, and the comfort and
encouragement of pilgrims.

The next day they took Christian into the armoury. There
they showed him all kinds of equipment which their Lord
had provided for pilgrims: sword, shield, helmet, breast-
plate, all-prayer and shoes that would not wear out (Eph.
6:13–17). And there was enough to equip as many men for
the service of their Lord as there were stars in the sky.

Christian is made to see ancient things

They also showed Christian some of the implements with which the Lord's servants had done wonderful things. They showed him Moses' rod; the hammer and tent-peg with which Jael had killed Sisera (Judg. 4:21); the jars, trumpets and torches, too, with which Gideon had routed the armies of the Midianites (Judg. 8:1–25). They also showed him the ox-goad with which Shamgar struck down six hundred men (Judg. 3:31), the jawbone with which Samson did such mighty feats (Judg. 15:15–17), and the stone and the sling with which David killed Goliath of Gath (1 Sam. 17); also the sword with which their Lord will kill the man of sin on the day when he rises up to the prey. Besides this there were many other excellent things and all these gave Christian considerable delight. After this they rested again.

Christian is shown the Delectable Mountains

Then I saw in my dream that the next day Christian got up to travel on but they wanted him to stay another day. They said that if the day was clear they would show Christian the Delectable Mountains, which would encourage him even further because they were nearer his desired haven than the place he was in at present. So he agreed and stayed.

When the morning came they took him to the top of the house and told him to look to the south. And what a sight! A great distance away he saw a most pleasant mountainous country (Isa. 33:16–17), beautifully wooded, with vineyards and many kinds of fruit and also flowers, springs and fountains, delightful to look at. Then Christian asked the name of that country and they said it was Emmanuel's land.

'It is as open,' they said, 'as this hill is to all pilgrims. When you arrive there, you can see in front of you the gate of the Celestial City. The shepherds who live there will point it out.'

Christian sent away armed

Now Christian thought again about setting out and they agreed that he should. 'But first,' they said, 'let's go once again into the armoury.'

There they dressed Christian from head to foot in a suit of tried and tested armour, in case he was attacked on the way. Thus equipped for his journey, he walked to the gate with his friends. Once there he asked the porter if he'd seen any pilgrims pass by. The porter replied that he'd seen one.

'Did you know him?' asked Christian.

'I asked his name, and he told me it was Faithful,' said the porter.

'Oh, I know him,' said Christian. 'He's a close neighbour. He comes from the town where I was born. How far ahead do you think he is?'

'He'd have got below the hill by now.'

'Well, friend,' said Christian, 'the Lord be with you and may he add to all your blessings for the kindness that you've shown me.'

Then Christian went forward. Discretion, Piety, Charity and Prudence wanted to go with him down to the foot of the hill. So they walked together, going over their earlier conversations, till they came to the downward slope. Then Christian said that it had been difficult coming up, and as far as he could see it was dangerous going down.

'Yes,' said Prudence, 'it is. It's hard for a man to go down into the Valley of Humiliation, as you are about to, and not slip on the path. That's why we've come out to go with you.'

So Christian began his descent, but very warily. Despite this, he did slip once or twice.

Then I saw in my dream that when they reached the bottom of the hill these good companions gave Christian a loaf of bread, a bottle of wine, and a cluster of raisins, and Christian went on his way.

9

Apollyon

But now, in this Valley of Humiliation, poor Christian was hard put to it. He'd hardly gone a short distance before he saw an evil fiend, whose name is Apollyon, coming over the field to meet him (Rev. 9:11). Christian began to be afraid, and wondered whether to go back or to stand his ground. But he remembered that he had no armour on his back and thought that by turning his back he might give the fiend the advantage since then Apollyon could easily pierce him with his darts. So Christian resolved to go out and stand his ground. 'For,' he thought, 'if all I wanted to do was save my own life, that would still be the best way to stand.'

So he went forward and Apollyon met him. Now the monster was a hideous sight. He was covered with scales like a fish (they are his pride). He had wings like a dragon, feet like a bear, out of his belly billowed fire and smoke, and his mouth was like a lion's. When he had come up to Christian he looked at him scornfully.

'Where're you from and where're you going?' asked Apollyon.

'I'm from the City of Destruction, which is a centre of all evil, and I'm going to the City of Zion,' replied Christian.

'So, I see you're one of my subjects; all that country is mine, and I'm its prince and god (2 Cor. 4:4). Why have you run away from your ruler? If it weren't that I want you to do more work for me I'd strike you to the ground with a single blow right now.'

'It's true I was born in your dominion,' said Christian,

'but your service was hard, and it was impossible to live on the wages you pay, "for the wages of sin is death" (Rom. 6:23). So when I reached maturity, like other thoughtful people I looked around to see if I could do better.'

'No prince lets subjects go so easily,' said Apollyon, 'and neither will I let you. But since you complain of your work and wages, if you'll go back I here and now promise to give you what our country can afford.'

'But I've given myself over to another, in fact to the King of princes. How can I in all fairness go back to you?'

'You've done as the proverb says and "changed a bad for a worse",' replied Apollyon. 'But it's usual for those who've professed themselves his servants to give him the slip after a while and return to me. You do that too and everything will be fine.'

Christian then said, 'I've given him my loyalty and sworn allegiance to him. How can I go back on this and not be hanged as a traitor?'

Apollyon answered, 'You did the same to me, and yet even now I'm willing to overlook it all if you'll turn round again and return to me.'

'What I promised you I did when I was under age, and besides, I believe that the Prince under whose banner I now stand is able to absolve me. Yes, and to forgive everything I did when I obeyed you. Besides, you destroyer Apollyon, to tell the truth I like his service, I like his wages, his servants, his government, his company, and his country better than yours. So stop trying to persuade me any further. I'm his servant, and I'll follow him.'

'Think again, Christian, when you're calmer. Think what you're likely to meet with on the path you're heading. You know that for the most part his servants come to a sticky end because they go against me and my ways. How many of them have been put to shameful deaths? Anyway, you say you believe his service to be better than mine when in fact he's never yet emerged from the place where he lives to deliver his servants from my grip. Yet, as for me, how many times, as all the world very well knows, have I come and by force or deceit delivered those who've faithfully served me, but have been taken by him. And so I will deliver you, too.'

'When he holds back from delivering them immediately it is on purpose, to test their love, and see if they will cling to him to the very end. As for the bad end you say they come to, for them it's glorious. They're not expecting to be delivered in the present. They're waiting for their glory, and shall have it when their Prince comes in his glory and the glory of the angels.'

'You've already been unfaithful in your service to him, so what makes you think you'll receive any wages from him?' asked the fiend.

'How have I been unfaithful to him?'

'You lost heart when you first set out, when you almost choked in the pit of Despond. You tried wrong ways to get rid of your burden when you should have waited for your Prince to take it off. You sinfully fell asleep and lost your prized possession. You were almost persuaded to go back at the sight of the lions. And when you talk of your journey, and of what you've heard and seen, you're inwardly longing to be praised for all you've said and done.'

'This is all true, and much more which you've left out. But the Prince whom I serve and honour is merciful and ready to forgive. Besides, these weaknesses took hold of me in your territory. For there I sucked them in and I've since groaned under them in sorrow and have received forgiveness from my Prince.'

Apollyon in a rage falls upon Christian

Then Apollyon broke out into a terrible rage. 'I'm an enemy of this Prince. I hate who he is, his laws, and his people. I've come out on purpose to stop you.'

'Apollyon, beware what you do. For I'm in the King's highway, the way of holiness. So watch out for yourself.'

Then Apollyon straddled the whole width of the path and said, 'I'm devoid of fear. Prepare to die. For I swear by my infernal den that you'll go no further. Here I'll spill your soul.'

And with that Apollyon threw a flaming arrow at Christian's breast. But Christian was holding a shield. With the shield he deflected the arrow and so avoided that danger.

Then Christian began to fight, for he saw it was time to do something. Apollyon at first went for him, throwing arrows as thick as hail, and in spite of all Christian could do, Apollyon wounded him in his head, his hand and foot. This made Christian draw back a little. At this Apollyon followed up his attack, but Christian once again took courage and resisted as manfully as he could. This intense combat lasted for about half a day, till Christian was almost spent. For, as you will realise, Christian's wounds made him grow weaker and weaker.

So Apollyon, seeing his opportunity, closed in on Christian, and wrestling with him threw him in a dreadful fall. With that Christian's sword flew out of his hand. Then Apollyon said, 'I've got you now' and pressed hard to the kill so that Christian began to despair of life.

Christian's victory over Apollyon

But, as God would have it, while Apollyon was drawing himself up for his final blow in order to make an end of this good man, Christian quickly reached out for his sword, grasped it and said, 'Do not gloat over me, my enemy! Though I have fallen, I will rise' (Mic. 7:8). With that he gave Apollyon a deadly thrust which made him give way like someone who's received a fatal wound. Christian saw that and struck at him again, saying, 'No, in all these things we are more than conquerors through him who loved us.' (Rom. 8:37–9; Jas. 4:7). At that Apollyon spread out his dragon's wings and fled. And Christian did not see him again.

Unless you've seen and heard it for yourself, as I did, you cannot possibly imagine the yelling and hideous roaring that came from Apollyon throughout the fight. He sounded like a dragon. On the other hand, what sighs and groans burst from Christian's heart! In all that time I never caught so much as one happy expression on Christian's face. Only when he saw that he had wounded Apollyon with his two-edged sword did he smile and look up! It was the most dreadful scene that ever I saw.

When the battle was over Christian said, 'Here I will offer thanks to him who has delivered me out of the mouth of the lion, I'll thank the one who helped me against Apollyon. And so he did, saying,

> Great Beelzebub, the captain of this fiend,
> Design'd my ruin; therefore to this end
> He sent him harness'd out; and he with rage,
> That hellish was, did fiercely me engage.
> But blessed Michael helped me, and I
> By dint of sword did quickly make him fly:
> Therefore to him let me give lasting praise,
> And thank and bless his holy name always.

Then a hand appeared offering him some leaves from the 'tree of life' (Rev. 22:2). Christian took them, and applied them to the wounds that he'd received in the battle, and he was healed immediately. He also sat down in that place to eat some bread and drink from the bottle that he'd been given a little while before. When he was refreshed he continued on his journey with his drawn sword in his hand. As he said, 'For all I know some other enemy may be close by.' But he met with no further assault from Apollyon throughout the length of this valley.

10

The Valley of the Shadow of Death

Now at the end of this valley lay another valley, called the Valley of the Shadow of Death, and Christian had to go through it, because the path to the Celestial City passed right through the middle of it. Now this valley is a very lonely place. The prophet Jeremiah describes it as 'the barren wilderness . . . a land of deserts and rifts, a land of drought and darkness, a land where no-one travels and no-one lives' (Jer. 2:6).

Here Christian was worse put to it than in his fight with Apollyon, as you will see from this sequel.

I saw in my dream that as Christian got to the borders of the Shadow of Death two men met him who were hastily returning. They were sons of those who had brought an evil report of the good land (Num. 13). Christian spoke to them like this:

'Where're you going?'

'Back! Back! And we'd advise you to do the same, if you prize either life or peace.'

'Why? What's the matter?' asked Christian.

'Matter!' they said. 'We were going the same way as you, and went as far as we dare, in fact we were almost past the point of no return, because had we gone a little further we wouldn't be here to bring you the news.'

'But what did you meet?' asked Christian.

'Why, we were almost in the Valley of the Shadow of Death, but luckily we glanced ahead, and saw the danger before we came to it' (Ps. 44:19).

'But what have you seen?'

'Seen! We've seen the Valley itself. It's pitch-black. And we've seen hobgoblins, satyrs, and dragons of the pit, and we've heard continual howling and yelling, as if from people in unutterable misery, sitting bound in irons, and in great pain. And above that valley hang the discouraging clouds of confusion, and Death perpetually spreads his wings over it all. In a word, it's entirely dreadful, utterly without any order' (Job 3:5; 10:22).

Then Christian said, 'Nothing that you've said so far indicates that this is not my way to the desired haven.'

'It may be your way, but it's not ours.'

So they parted. Christian went on his way, still with drawn sword in hand for fear of another assault.

Then in my dream I saw that along the length of this valley on the right-hand side there was a very deep ditch. That is the ditch into which the blind have led the blind throughout all ages and where they have both miserably perished. Again, I saw on the left-hand side a very dangerous quagmire. Even a good man who falls into that will find no bottom for his feet. Into that mire King David once fell, and would no doubt have been smothered, if the one who is able had not plucked him out (Ps. 69:14).

The pathway here was extremely narrow so good Christian was in even greater difficulties. When he tried, in the dark, to shun the ditch on the one side he almost slipped into the mire on the other side, and when he tried to avoid the mire, it needed extreme care not to fall into the ditch. In this way he went on and I heard him sigh bitterly, for besides the dangers mentioned above the pathway here was so dark that often when he lifted up his foot to walk forward he didn't know where, or on what, he would be setting it down.

About the middle of the valley and close to the path, I saw the mouth of hell. Now Christian wondered what to do. Every so often the flame and smoke would belch out thickly, with sparks and hideous noises. Unlike Apollyon, such things were indifferent to Christian's sword so he was forced to sheathe his sword, and take up another weapon, called All-prayer (Eph. 6:18). I heard him cry, 'O Lord, save me' (Ps. 116:4). He went on like this a long time, but still the flames reached towards him. He heard, too, mournful voices and rushings, forwards and backwards, so that sometimes he imagined he'd be torn in pieces, or trodden underfoot like the filth in the streets.

For several miles, Christian saw this frightful sight and heard these dreadful noises. At a place where he thought he heard a company of fiends coming to meet him, he stopped and began to think what it was best to do. Sometimes he was in half a mind to go back, but then again he thought he might be half-way through the valley. He recalled how he had already overcome many dangers, and that it might be more dangerous to go back than to go forward. So he resolved to go on. Yet the fiends seemed to come nearer. When they were almost on him, he cried out, 'I will walk in the strength of the Lord God.' At this they dropped back and came no closer. One thing I must not omit: I noticed that poor Christian was now so confused that he didn't know his own voice. Just as he was by the mouth of the burning pit one of the wicked ones got behind him and whispered many serious blasphemies to him, which he honestly thought had come from his own mind. Christian was more put out by this than by anything else he had met with so far. It upset him even to think that he should now blaspheme the one he had loved so much. Yet if he could have helped it, he wouldn't have done it: but he lacked the wisdom either to stop listening, or to recognise where those blasphemies came from.

When Christian had travelled in this unhappy state for some considerable time, he thought he heard the voice of a man that seemed to be going before him, saying, 'Even though I walk through the valley of the shadow of death, I will fear no evil, for you are with me' (Ps. 23:4).

Then Christian was glad and for three reasons: first, because he realised that others who feared God were in this valley, as well as himself. Second, because he saw that God was with them, despite that dark and dismal situation, and therefore why not with him, too, even though he was prevented from seeing him by the sort of place it was (Job 9:11). Third, he was glad because he hoped that if he overtook them he would have company. So he went on, and called out to the one who was ahead, though he didn't know what to say, because he also thought he was alone.

In time, day came. Then Christian said, 'He turns blackness into dawn' (Amos 5:8).

Now that it was morning, Christian looked back, not from a desire to return, but to see by the light of the day just what hazards he had gone through in the dark. He saw more clearly the ditch that was on one side, and the mire that was on the other. He also saw how narrow the path was between them both. Now he saw too, the hobgoblins, the satyrs, and dragons of the pit, but all at a distance because with the break of the day they stayed away. Yet they were revealed to him, as it is written, 'He reveals the deep things of darkness and brings deep shadows into the light' (Job 12:22).

The second part of this valley is very dangerous

Now Christian was very moved by his deliverance from all the dangers of his solitary way. Though he had been more afraid of them earlier, he now saw them more clearly, because the light of the day made them stand out. About this time the sun was rising, which was another blessing. You must note that though the first part of the Valley of the Shadow of Death was dangerous, this second part, which Christian had still to travel, was, if possible, even more dangerous. The entire length of the path from the place where Christian now stood right to the end of the valley, was set so full of snares, traps, gins, and nets, on the one hand, and pits, pitfalls, deep holes, and shelvings on the other, that had it still been dark, even if he had had a thousand souls, you could reasonably expect them to have been cast away. But, as I just said, the sun was rising.

Then Christian said, 'His lamp shone upon my head and by his light I walked through darkness!' (Job 29:3).

In this light, then, he came to the end of the valley.

Now in my dream I saw that at the end of this valley lay blood, bones, ashes and mangled bodies of men and pilgrims who had previously gone this way. While I was pondering over the reason for this, I caught sight of a cave a little way ahead, where two giants, Pope and Pagan, had lived in olden times. It was by their power and tyranny that men whose bones, blood and ashes were lying there, were cruelly put to death. Christian went through without much danger which puzzled me rather, but I have since learnt that Pagan has been dead a long time, and the Pope, though still alive, is so old and had so many close shaves when he was younger, that he has grown crazy and stiff in his joints, and can do little more than sit in his cave's mouth, glaring at pilgrims as they go by, and biting his nails because he can't get at them.

So I saw Christian continue on his way. And when he saw the old man sitting in the mouth of the cave, he didn't know what to think, especially when Pope, though unable to go after him, said, 'You'll never be put right till more of you are burned.'

But Christian held his peace, and put a good face on it. So he passed by and came to no harm. Then Christian sang,

> Oh, world of wonders! (I can say no less)
> That I should be preserved in that distress
> That I have met with here! Oh, blessed be
> The hand that hath from it delivered me!
> Dangers in darkness, devils, hell, and sin,
> Did compass me while I this vale was in:
> Yea, snares, and pits, and traps, and nets did lie
> My path about, that worthless, silly I

Might have been catch'd, entangled, and cast down:
But since I live, let Jesus wear the crown.

11

Christian and Faithful

As Christian went on he came to a small rise in the ground that had been made on purpose so that pilgrims might see ahead. Christian climbed up and looking forward he saw Faithful ahead of him on his journey. Christian called aloud, 'Hey! Hey! Wait! I'll be your companion.' At that Faithful looked behind him and Christian called again, 'Wait! Wait, till I catch up with you.'

But Faithful answered, 'No! My life is at stake, and the avenger of blood is behind me.'

Christian was moved by this, and exerting all his strength he quickly caught up with Faithful, and then overtook him, so that the last was first. Then Christian gave a conceited smile, because he had got ahead of his brother. But not paying careful attention to his feet, he suddenly stumbled and fell and couldn't get up again until Faithful came to help him.

Then I saw in my dream that they went on talking very lovingly together of all the things that had happened to them on their pilgrimage.

Christian began: 'My honoured and dear brother Faithful, I am glad that I've caught up with you, and that God has prepared our spirits so that we can be companions on this very pleasant path.'

'I had thought, dear friend, to have had your company right from our town,' Faithful said. 'But you got the start of me and I was forced to come much of the way alone.'

'How long did you stay in the City of Destruction, before

you set out after me?' asked Christian.

'Till I could stay no longer. Soon after you left there was much talk that our city would soon be burned down to the ground with fire from heaven.'

'What! Did your neighbours say this?'

'Yes, for a while it was on everybody's lips.'

'What! And did no one but you come out to escape the danger?'

'Yes. Though there was a great deal of talk, I don't think they really believed it because in the heat of conversation I heard some of them speak scathingly of you, and of your *desperate journey* – or so they called your pilgrimage. But I believed it, and I still believe that the end of our city will come with fire and sulphur from above. And therefore I've made my escape.'

'Did you hear nothing about our neighbour Pliable?'

'Yes, I heard that he followed you till he came to the Slough of Despond, where some say he fell in – though he wouldn't admit to it. But I must say he was filthy with that sort of muck.'

'And what did his neighbours say to him?'

'Since his return he's been an object of derision – and among all sorts of people. Some ridicule and despise him, and hardly anyone will employ him. He's now seven times worse off than if he'd never left the city.'

'But they despised the path that he abandoned, so why were they so set against him?'

'Oh! They say, "Hang him!" He's a turncoat. He wasn't true to what he professed to believe. I think even God's enemies have been stirred up by God to scorn Pliable and make him a byword to everyone (Jer. 29:18–19), because he's abandoned the way.'

'Didn't you talk to him before you left?'

'I met him once in the street, but he sidled away on the other side like someone who's ashamed, so I didn't speak to him.'

'Well,' said Christian, 'when I first set out, I had hopes of that man, but now I'm afraid he'll perish when the city is destroyed, for, "Of them the proverbs are true: 'A dog returns to its vomit,' and, 'A sow that is washed goes back to her wallowing in the mud'" (2 Pet. 2:22).'

'Those are my fears, too, but who can stop what is meant to be?'

'Well, Faithful, let's forget about him, and talk about things that concern us,' said Christian. 'Tell me what you encountered as you came along: I know you must have, it would be a marvel if you met nothing at all.'

Faithful attacked by Wanton

'I escaped the bog that I see you fell into and got to the gate without having to face that danger, only I met someone called Wanton who could well have caused me great harm.'

'It was a good thing you escaped her net. Joseph was given a hard time by her, and he escaped, just as you did, but it nearly cost him his life (Gen. 39:11–13). But what did she do to you?'

'Unless you've experienced something of her you can't imagine what a flattering tongue she has. She put all she'd got into enticing me to go with her, promising me every sort of happiness.'

'No – she couldn't promise you the happiness a good conscience brings.'

'You know what I mean. All worldly and physical happiness.'

'Thank God you escaped her: "The mouth of an adulteress is a deep pit; he who is under the Lord's wrath will fall into it"' (Prov. 22:14).

'No, I'm not sure I did entirely escape her.'

'Why? I'm sure you didn't give in to her.'

'No, not to pollute myself. I remembered some old words I had seen that said "her steps lead straight to the grave" (Prov. 5:5). So I closed my eyes because I would not be bewitched by her looks. Then she ranted and raved at me and I went on' (Job 31:1).

'Did you meet any other attack as you came?'

'When I came to the foot of the Hill called Difficulty, I met a very old man who asked me who I was, and where I was going. I told him that I was a pilgrim going to the Celestial City. So he said, "You look an honest chap. Would you like to live with me and accept the wages that I give you?" So I asked him his name, and where he lived and he said his name was Adam the First, and he lived in the town of Deceit (Eph. 4:22). I asked him what his work was, and what wages he would give. He told me that his work was many delights, and for payment, I would be his heir. Then I asked him what his house was like, and what other servants he had. He told me that his house was provided with all the dainties in the world, and his servants were his own children. I asked how many children he had and he said that he had only three daughters: "the Cravings of sinful man, the Lust of the eyes, and the Boasting of what he has and does" (1 John 2:16). He told me I could marry them if I wanted. I asked how long he wanted me to live with him and he told me as long as he lived himself.'

'Well – what conclusion did you both come to?'

'At first I found myself a bit inclined to go with the man. I thought he spoke very reasonably, but then as I was talking to him I looked at his forehead, and written there I saw the words, "take off your old self with its practices"' (Col. 3:9).

'What then?'

'Then it burnt hot into my mind that whatever he said and however much he flattered, when he got me home to his house he would sell me as a slave. So I asked him to stop talking because I wouldn't go near the door of his house. Then he abused me, and told me he would send someone after me who would make me hate the way I was going. So I turned to go away from him. But just as I turned to go I felt him take hold of my flesh, and give me such a deadly pinch that I thought he'd pulled part of me back to himself. This made me cry out, "What a wretched man I am!" (Rom.

7:24). But I went on my way up the hill. When I'd got about half-way up, I looked behind and saw someone coming after me, as swift as the wind. He overtook me just at the place where the bench stands.'

Christian interrupted, 'I sat down to rest just there myself, but was overcome with sleep, and I lost this scroll from out of my breast pocket.'

'Listen. Let me finish. No sooner had the man overtaken me than with just a word and a blow, he knocked me down, and I was laid out for dead. But when I had revived a little I asked him why he had treated me like that. He said it was because of my secret leaning towards Adam the First, and with that he struck me another deadly blow on the chest, and beat me down backwards. So again I lay at his feet as if dead. When I came to again I cried to him for mercy. But he said, "I don't know how to show mercy." And with that he knocked me down again. He would doubtless have finished me off except that someone came by and asked him to leave off.'

'Who was that?' asked Christian?

'I didn't know him at first, but as he passed I saw the holes in his hands and in his side, and then I realised that he was our Lord. So I went up the hill.'

'That man who overtook you was Moses,' Christian said. 'He doesn't spare anyone, nor does he know how to show mercy to those who break his law.'

'How well I know it,' Faithful agreed. 'That wasn't the first time I've come across him. It was he who came to me when I lived safely at home and told me he would burn my house over my head if I stayed there.'

'But didn't you see the house that stood on the top of that hill where Moses met you?'

'I did,' said Faithful, 'and the lions before I came to the house. But I think the lions were asleep, for it was about noon, and because I had so much of the day still before me I passed by the porter and came down the hill.'

'Yes, the porter told me that he saw you go by. But I wish

you'd called at the house. They would have shown you so many rare things that you could scarcely have forgotten them till your dying day. But, tell me, did you meet nobody in the Valley of Humility?'

Faithful attacked by Discontent

'Yes,' said Faithful, 'I met someone called Discontent. He would have been only too glad if he could have persuaded me to return with him. His reason was that the valley was altogether without honour. He also told me that going there would annoy my friends Pride, Arrogance, Self-conceit, Worldly-glory, and others whom he knew. He said they would be extremely offended if I made such a fool of myself as to wade through that valley.'

'Well, and how did you reply to him?'

Faithful's answer to Discontent

'I told Discontent that all the people he'd named might claim to be relations of mine, and rightly so, for they were my blood relations, but they'd disowned me when I became a pilgrim, and I'd rejected them, too. So they now meant no more than if we'd never been related. I told him, too, that as far as this valley was concerned he'd totally misrepresented it, for "humility comes before honour" and "a haughty spirit before a fall" (Prov. 15:33; 16:18). Therefore, said I, I'd rather go through this valley for the honour acknowledged by the wisest, than choose what Discontent deemed most worthy of our love.'

'And you met with nothing else in that valley?' probed Christian.

Faithful is attacked by Shame

'Well I did,' said Faithful. 'I met with Shame. But out of all the men that I've met on my pilgrimage, he, I think, bears the wrong name. Others would accept a refusal after a bit of arguing or whatever, but not this bold-faced Shame.'

'Why, what did he say to you?' asked Christian.

'Say! Why he objected to religion itself. He said it was a pathetic, feeble, snivelling activity for a man. He said a tender conscience was effeminate and that for a man to have to watch his words and actions and tie himself up so that he couldn't speak with the bold liberty which the brave spirits of the times are used to, would make him the laughing stock of society. He objected, too, because he said very few of the mighty, rich, or wise were ever of my opinion (John 7:48; 1 Cor. 1:26), in fact, none of them was, until they were persuaded to be fools (1 Cor. 3:18; Phil. 3:7–9), and to stupidly risk losing everything for who knows what. He also objected to the inferior and humble lifestyle and status of most of the pilgrims and pointed out their ignorance and lack of understanding of all natural sciences. (John 7:48). Honestly, he went on at me like that about a great many more things than I'm telling you. Like, how shameful it was to sit whining and mourning under a sermon, and how shameful to come home sighing and groaning; that it was shameful to ask my neighbour to forgive me for petty faults, or to repay anything I'd taken from anyone. Also he said religion made a man turn away from great people just because they had a few vices (which he called by finer names), and made him acknowledge and respect worthless types just because they were of the same religious fellowship. And wasn't that shameful?' he said.

'And what did you say to him?' Christian asked.

'Say! I couldn't think what to say at first. Honestly! He made me feel so embarrassed that I went quite red. Shame made me blush, and had me almost beaten. But at last I began to consider that "What is highly valued among men is detestable in God's sight" (Luke 16:15). And I thought again that this Shame tells me what men are but tells me nothing about what God or the word of God is. And what's more I thought that at the Day of Destruction we'll not be doomed to death or life according to what the hectoring spirits of the world say, but according to the wisdom and law of the Highest. So I thought that what God says is best, yes *is* best, even though the whole world is against it. Seeing, then, that God prefers religion, and a tender conscience, and seeing that those who make themselves fools for the kingdom of heaven are wisest, and that the poor man who loves Christ is richer than the greatest man in the world who hates Christ, then Shame, be gone, for you are an enemy of my salvation. Shall I entertain Shame instead of my sovereign Lord? Then how will I look him in the face when he comes? If I'm ashamed of his ways and his servants now, how can I expect the blessing? (Mark 8:38). But I must say this Shame was a barefaced scoundrel. I could hardly shake him off. Honestly, he insisted on haunting me. He kept whispering in my ear, bringing up one or other of the weaknesses of religion. At last I told him that it was useless to try anything else because I saw most glory in the very things he scorned. And so finally I got away from this shameless creature. And when I'd shaken him off, I began to sing:

> The trials that those men do meet withal,
> That are obedient to the heavenly call,
> Are manifold, and suited to the flesh,
> And come, and come, and come again afresh.
> That now, or some time else, we by them may
> Be taken, overcome, and cast away.
> Oh, let the pilgrims, let the pilgrims then
> Be vigilant and quit themselves like men.'

'I'm glad, brother,' said Christian, that you withstood this scoundrel so bravely. As you say, out of everyone, I think he has the wrong name. For he's so barefaced that he follows us in the streets, and tries to put us to shame in full view of everyone. He tries to make us ashamed of what is good, and if he himself were not audacious, he'd never attempt to act as he does. But let's continue to resist him, for despite all his bravado, he encourages only the fool, and no one else. "The wise inherit honour," said Solomon, "but fools he holds up to shame"' (Prov. 3:35).

'Yes,' Faithful said, 'I think we must cry for help against Shame to the one who would have us be valiant for truth on the earth.'

'What you say is true, but did you meet nobody else in that valley?'

'No, I didn't, for I had sunshine all the rest of the way, and also through the Valley of the Shadow of Death,' replied Faithful.

'That was good. It was quite the opposite for me. Almost as soon as I entered that valley, I had a long and dreadful fight with that foul fiend Apollyon. Honestly, I really thought he was going to kill me, especially when he got me down and crushed me under him, as if he was going to crush me to pieces. You see, as he threw me, my sword flew out of my hand and in fact he told me he was sure of me. But I called to God, and he heard me, and saved me out of all my troubles (Ps. 34:6). Then I entered the Valley of the Shadow of Death, and had no light for almost half the way through. I thought I'd be killed over and over again. But at last day broke, and the sun rose, and I went through what was left far more easily and quietly.'

12

Talkative

And then I saw in my dream that as they went on Faithful
happened to look to one side and saw a man, whose name
is Talkative, walking a little way from them, for there was
enough room for them all to walk there. He was a tall man,
and rather more good-looking at a distance than close at
hand. Faithful spoke to this man as follows.

Faithful and Talkative talk to each other

'Where're you off to? Are you going to the heavenly country?' Faithful asked.

'I'm going to that very place,' replied Talkative.

'Good, then I hope we may have the pleasure of your
company,' said Faithful.

'I'll be very glad to go with you.'

'Come on, then, let's go on together, and spend our time
talking about worthwhile things.'

'I'm only too pleased to talk about things that are good –
either with you or anyone else. And I'm very glad that I've
met up with those who are inclined to such a good occupation. For, to tell the truth, very few people care to spend
their time like this as they travel. They'd much rather talk
aimlessly about nothing. And this has troubled me.'

'That's most certainly something to be regretted. And
what more worthwhile things could men on earth talk about
than the things of the God of heaven?' asked Faithful.

'I like you enormously because you speak with conviction,' Talkative said. 'And, yes, what could be more pleasant, or valuable than to talk of the things of God? Is there anything more pleasant – that is, to someone who delights in wonderful things? For example, if a man delights in talking of the history or the mystery of things, or loves to talk of miracles, wonders, or signs, where could he find them recorded in a more delightful way, or more pleasingly expressed, than in the Holy Scriptures?'

'That's true. But in all our talk it should be our aim to benefit from such things.'

'That's what I said,' said Talkative. 'Because talking about such things is most beneficial. By talking a man may gain knowledge of many things, such as the emptiness of earthly things, and the worth of heavenly things. That's the general point. In particular, in this way a man may learn the necessity of the new birth, the insufficiency of our works, the need of Christ's righteousness, and so on. However, as he talks about these things he may learn what it is to repent, to believe, to pray, to suffer, and such like. He may also learn what are the great promises and encouragements of the gospel. In addition, he may learn to refute false opinions, to vindicate the truth, and to instruct the ignorant.'

'This is so true, and I'm glad to hear you say these things,' said Faithful.

'It's so sad,' sighed Talkative. 'Our failure to talk in this way is the reason why so few understand the need for faith, and the necessity of a work of grace in their soul in order to possess eternal life. It's why so many ignorantly live under the works of the law by which no man can ever obtain the kingdom of heaven.'

'But if I may say so,' queried Faithful, 'heavenly knowledge of such things is the gift of God. No one acquires understanding by human effort, or just by talking of it.'

'I know all this only too well,' replied Talkative. 'A man can receive nothing unless it is given him from heaven. All is by grace, not works. I could quote you a hundred scriptures to confirm this.'

'Well, then,' said Faithful, 'what in particular shall we talk about just now?'

'Whatever you like. I'll talk of heavenly things or earthly things, moral things or evangelical things, sacred things or profane things, past things or things to come, foreign things or things at home, more essential things or peripheral things. Anything, provided it is all to our benefit.'

Faithful charmed by Talkative

Now Faithful was most impressed, and stepping up to Christian who had walked all this while by himself, said to him softly, 'What a fine companion we've got! Surely this man will make a great pilgrim.'

At this, Christian gave a slight smile, and said, 'With that tongue of his this man you're so taken with will charm twenty people who don't know him.'

'Do you know him then?'

'Know him! Better than he knows himself.'

'Well who is he?' asked Faithful.

'His name is Talkative. He lives in our town. I'm amazed that you don't know him. But then I suppose our town is large.'

'Who's his father and where does he live?' probed Faithful.

'He's the son of Say-well, who lived in Prating-row, and he's known by all who are acquainted with him as Talkative of Prating-row. For all his fine tongue, he's a pathetic figure.'

'But he seems to be a very fine man,' said Faithful.

'Yes he is – to all who don't know him very well. He's at his best away from home, near home he's ugly enough. Your remark that he's a good-looking man brings to mind what I've observed in the work of some painters; their pictures show up best from a distance, but close to they're less pleasing.'

'But your smile makes me inclined to think that you're only joking,' said Faithful.

'God forbid that I should joke about such a thing, even though I smiled,' replied Christian. 'Or that I should accuse anyone falsely. I'll tell you something more about him. This man is all for any company and any talk. He'll talk at the pub just as enthusiastically as he's talked with you now, and the more drink in his head, the more words in his mouth! Religion has no real place in his heart, or home, or life. All he has is found on his tongue. His religion is to make a noise with it.'

'Do you mean that? Then I've been seriously deceived by this man,' Faithful said.

'Deceived! You can be sure of that! Remember the saying, "they do not practise what they preach" (Matt. 23:3). For "the kingdom of God is not a matter of talk but of power" (1 Cor. 4:20). He talks about prayer, and repentance, and faith, and the new birth, but he only knows how to talk about them. I've visited his family, and have observed him at home and outside, and I know what I'm saying is true. His home is as empty of religion as the white of an egg is of flavour. There's no prayer, or any sign of repentance for sin. It's true to say that a beast among beasts serves God far better than he does. To everyone who knows him he's a blot on our faith. He brings reproach and shame to the name of religion (Rom. 2:23–4). There's hardly a good word said about Christianity in all his part of the town – just because of him. People who know him say, "A saint abroad, and a devil at home." His poor family can vouch for that. He's so churlish, he rants and raves so much, and is so unreasonable with his servants that they never know what to do or how to speak to him. Those who have any dealings with him say it's better to do business with a Turk than with him. You'll get a fairer deal with a Turk than you'll get at his hands! If he possibly can this man Talkative will outdo them all. He'll defraud, cheat, and in every way get the better of them. What's more, he brings up his sons to follow in his footsteps. If he sees in them any trace of "stupid cowardice" (as he terms the first appearance of a tender conscience), he calls them fools and blockheads, and nothing will persuade him to give them a decent job, or to commend them to others. It's my view that by his wicked life he's caused many to stumble and fall, and if God doesn't stop him he'll be the ruin of many more,' concluded Christian.

'Well, brother, I'm bound to believe you, not just because you say you know him, but because you speak as a Christian. I can't believe that you say all these things out of ill-will. It must be exactly as you say,' said Faithful.

'Had I known no more of him than you,' said Christian, 'I might perhaps have come to your opinion. In fact, had I heard this report only from the enemies of religion, I'd have thought it mere slander – a lot of that falls from bad men's mouths on to good men's names and professions. But I can personally prove him guilty of all these things and a great many more just as bad. Besides, good men are ashamed of him. You don't find them calling him brother or friend. If they know him, the very mention of his name makes them blush.'

'Well, I can see that *saying* and *doing* are two different things, and from now on I'll observe this distinction better,' said Faithful.

'They're two different things indeed. They're as different as the soul and the body. For just as the body without the soul is a dead carcase, so *saying*, if it's alone, is no more than a dead carcase, too. The soul of religion is the practical part,' Christian continued. 'Religion that God our Father accepts as pure and faultless is this: to look after orphans and widows in their distress and to keep oneself from being polluted by the world (Jas. 1:22–7). This fellow Talkative is not aware of this. He thinks that hearing and saying make a good Christian, and so he deceives his own soul. Hearing is just the sowing of the seed; talking is not enough to prove that the fruit is actually in the heart and life. And be quite sure that at Judgment Day men will be judged according to their fruit. No one will say, "Did you believe?" but only, "Were you *doers* or *only talkers*?" and everyone will be judged accordingly. (See Matt. 13:23; 25:31–46.) The end of the world is compared to a harvest, and you know that at harvest time men are only interested in fruit. Not that anything can be accepted which is not of faith, but I'm saying this to show you how insignificant Talkative's profession of faith will be on that day.'

Faithful convinced of the badness of Talkative

Then Faithful said, 'This brings to my mind what Moses wrote when he described a beast that's clean. A clean beast has a split hoof, and chews the cud (Lev. 11; Deut. 14). He doesn't have only a split hoof and he doesn't only chew cud. The hare chews the cud, but is unclean because it doesn't have a split hoof as well. And this really does resemble Talkative. He chews the cud and seeks knowledge. He chews on the word, but he doesn't have a split hoof, and he doesn't separate himself from the way of sinners. He's like the hare with the foot of a dog, or bear. Therefore he's unclean.'

'For all I know,' said Christian, 'you've given the true gospel meaning of those texts, and I'll add another thing. Some men – and they're the ones who're great talkers, too – Paul calls "resounding gongs, and clanging cymbals", that is, as he expounds in another place, they're "lifeless things that make sounds" (1 Cor. 13:1–3; 14:7). In other words, they're lifeless, without the true faith and grace of the gospel, and consequently will never be placed in the kingdom of heaven among the children of life, even though their talk sounds like the tongue or voice of an angel.'

'Well,' Faithful said, 'I wasn't that fond of his company at first, and am quite sick of it now. What shall we do to get rid of him?'

'Take my advice, and do as I tell you, and you'll find that

he'll soon be sick of your company, too, unless God touches his heart and changes it.'

'What do you suggest I do?'

'Well, go to him, and enter into a serious discussion about the *power* of religion. When he's approved of it – as he will – ask him straight out whether this is found in his heart, home, or life.'

Then Faithful went forward again and spoke to Talkative. 'Well now? Any news? How're things?' he said.

'Very well, thank you,' said Talkative. 'I thought we'd have had a long chat by now.'

'Well, if you want, we can start now,' said Faithful, 'and since you left it up to me to propose the question, how about this: How does God's saving grace reveal itself when it's in a man's heart?'

'I see, then, that our talk is to be about the *power* of things. Well, it's a very good question. And I'm willing to give an answer. In brief, like this. First, where the grace of God is in the heart, it causes a great outcry against sin. Second ...'

'Hold on!' interrupted Faithful. 'Let's consider your points one at a time. I think you should rather say, "it shows itself by making the soul hate its sin".'

'Why, what difference is there between crying out against, and hating sin?'

'Oh! A great deal! A man may cry out against sin as a matter of policy, but he can't hate it unless he's been given a godly antipathy to it. I've heard many cry out against sin in the pulpit, who find it easy enough to live with in their heart, home, and life. Potiphar's wife cried out very loudly as if she were very holy, but for all that she would willingly have committed adultery with Joseph (Gen. 39:11–15). Many cry out against sin. Even a mother cries out against her child on her lap, when she calls it a bad, naughty girl, and then starts hugging and kissing it.'

'You're trying to catch me out, I can see,' Talkative said.

'No, I'm setting things right, that's all. But what would

you say is the second proof of a work of grace in the heart?'
asked Faithful.

'Great knowledge of gospel mysteries.'

Great knowledge is no sign of grace

'This sign should have been put first, but, first or last, it's
also false. It's possible to acquire knowledge – even great
knowledge of the mysteries of the gospel – without
experiencing any work of grace in the soul (1 Cor. 13). In
fact, if a man has all knowledge he may still amount to nothing, and so not be a child of God. When Christ said, "Do
you know all these things?" and the disciples answered,
"Yes", Christ added, "Blessed are you if you do them." He
doesn't lay the blessing on the *knowing* of these things, but
on the *doing* of them. For there's a knowledge that's not
accompanied by doing: a man may know his master's will
and not do it. He may know like an angel, and yet be no
Christian. Therefore your sign is not true. Indeed, to *know*
is a thing that pleases the talker and boaster, but to *do* is
what pleases God. Not that the heart can be good without
knowledge, for without knowledge the heart is nothing.
But there is knowledge and knowledge. One kind of knowledge consists of mere speculation about things, and
another kind of knowledge is accompanied by the grace of
faith and love, and sets a man doing the will of God from
the heart. The first of these kinds will satisfy the talker. But
the true Christian is not content without the other kind.
"Give me understanding, and I will keep your law and obey
it with all my heart"' (Ps. 119:34).

'You're trying to trap me again. This isn't constructive.'

'Well, please suggest another indication of this work of
grace.'

'Not me. I can see we won't agree,' said Talkative.

'Well, if you won't, will you allow me to do so?'

'Feel free!'

The work of grace in a soul

So Faithful began, 'A work of grace in a soul reveals itself, both to the one who has it and to the observer. To the one who has it, it brings conviction of sin. He's especially convicted about the corruption of his nature, and his sin of unbelief, for which he's certain to be damned, if he doesn't find mercy at God's hand through faith in Jesus Christ (Ps. 38:18; Mark 16:16; John 16:8–9; Acts 4:12; Rom. 7:24.) This sight and knowledge bring sorrow and shame. But he finds, also, that the Saviour of the world is revealed to him, together with the absolute necessity of being united to him for life. And he finds that he hungers and thirsts for his Saviour and it's for this hunger and thirst that the promise is given (Jer. 31:19; Matt. 5:6; Gal. 1:15–16; Rev. 21:6). According to the strength or weakness of his faith in his Saviour, so are his joy and peace, his love of holiness, his desire to know him more, and to serve him in this world.

'But though, as I say,' continued Faithful, 'grace reveals itself to him like this, only seldom does he realise that this is a work of grace. This is because his present corruption and his misused reason, make his mind judge wrongly. A very sound judgment is required before anyone can come to a firm conclusion that grace is at work within him.

'To others the work of grace is revealed in this way. First, when someone testifies that he has experienced faith in Christ; second, by a life matching up to that testimony. This is a life of holiness – heart-holiness, family-holiness (if he has a family), and by holiness in the way he lives in the world. This holiness teaches him to detest this sin, and hate himself for his own secret sins, to suppress sin in his family, and to promote holiness in the world, not just by talk as a hypocrite or talkative person may do, but by actually subjecting everything, in faith and love, to the power of the word (Job 42:5–6; Ps. 50:23; Ezek. 20:43; Matt. 5:8; John 14:15; Rom. 10:9–10;

Phil. 1:27). And now, sir, with regard to this brief description of the work of grace, and the way it's revealed, if you have anything against all this, then object; if not, allow me leave to put a second question to you.'

'No, no,' said Talkative, 'my job now is not to object but to listen. Let's have your second question.'

'It's this: do you experience the first part of this description of grace? And do your life and behaviour testify to it? Or is your religion based on word and tongue, and not on deed and truth? If you feel inclined to give me an answer, please don't say any more than you know God above will say Amen to. Say nothing that your conscience cannot confirm, "for not he that commends himself is approved, but whom the Lord commends". Besides, to say I'm like this or that when my way of life denies it and all my neighbours tell me I'm lying is very wrong.'

At first Talkative began to blush. But recovering himself he replied, 'You've turned now to experience, to conscience, and God; and appeal to him in justification of what is said. I didn't expect this kind of discussion, nor do I feel disposed to answer such questions. I'm not bound to answer you – unless you were teaching me the catechism, and even then I may refuse to let you be my judge. But tell me why you're asking me such questions.'

'Because I saw you were quick to talk, and because I didn't know if there was anything more to you, apart from ideas. Besides, to tell you the whole truth, I've heard that you're a man whose religion consists of talk, and that your way of life belies what you profess with your mouth. They say you're a blot among Christians and that religion suffers because of your ungodly behaviour. They say that some have already stumbled because of your wicked ways, and that more are in danger of being destroyed by you. Your religion stands alongside your drinking, your greed for gain, immorality, swearing, lying, and the useless company you keep. That proverb about a prostitute which says, "she is a shame to all women", is true of you – you're a shame to all believers.

'Since you're so quick to pick up hearsay, and jump to hasty conclusions, I can only think that you're a bad-tempered, miserable so-and-so, not fit to talk to seriously. So, goodbye!'

Then Christian came up and said to his brother Faithful, 'I told you what would happen. Your words and his passions couldn't agree. He'd rather leave your company than change his ways. But he's gone, as I said. Let him go. The loss is no one's but his own. He's saved us the trouble of leaving him, for, if he goes on in the same way, as I suppose he will, he'd have been just a blot in our company. Besides, the apostle says, "From such withdraw yourself."'

'But I'm glad we had this little talk with him,' Faithful said. 'Maybe he'll think of it again. Anyway, I've spoken plainly to him, and so am clear of his blood if he dies.'

'You did well to talk as plainly to him as you did,' said Christian. 'There's very little of this kind of true dealing nowadays, and that makes religion stink in many people's nostrils. Many of these talkative fools, whose religion is only in words and whose lives are debauched and empty, are admitted into Christian fellowships and it makes people in the world stumble, blemishes Christianity, and grieves those who are sincere. I wish that everyone would deal with these types the way you have. Then they would either conform more closely to true religion, or the company of saints would become too hot for them.'

Then Faithful said:

> How Talkative at first lifts up his plumes!
> How bravely doth he speak! How he presumes
> To drive down all before him! But so soon
> As Faithful talks of heart-work, like the moon
> That's past the full, into the wane he goes:
> And so will all but he that heart-work knows.

So they went on their way talking of what they had seen, and that lightened a walk which would otherwise no doubt have been tedious for now they were travelling through a wilderness.

13

Vanity Fair

Now when they were almost out of this wilderness, Faithful chanced to glance back, and spotted someone following whom he knew. 'Oh!' said Faithful to his brother, 'Who's that coming over there?'

Christian looked up, and said, 'It's my good friend Evangelist.'

'And my good friend, too,' said Faithful. 'He's the one who put me on the path to the gate.'

Now Evangelist came up to them, and greeted them with the words: 'Success, success, to you, and success to those who help you!' (1 Chron. 12:18).

'Welcome, welcome, my good Evangelist,' said Christian. 'The sight of your face makes me remember your past kindness and your untiring work for my eternal good.'

'And a thousand times welcome,' said good Faithful. 'Your company, sweet Evangelist, is most welcome to us poor pilgrims!'

Then Evangelist said, 'How has it gone with you, friends, since we parted? What have you met, and how have you behaved?'

Then Christian and Faithful told Evangelist about all the things that had happened to them on the way, and how, and with what difficulty, they had arrived at that place.

Evangelist's exhortation to Faithful and Christian

'I'm truly glad,' said Evangelist, 'not that you've met with trials, but that you've come out on top, and despite many weaknesses you've continued on the way to this very day. I'm truly glad for my own sake as well as yours. I've sowed and you've reaped, and the day is coming, when "the sower and the reaper may be glad together" (John 4:36): that is, if you hold out; "for at the proper time we will reap a harvest if we do not give up " (Gal. 6:9). The crown is before you and it's incorruptible, so "Run in such a way as to get the prize" (1 Cor. 9:24–7). There are some who set out for this crown, and after going a long way for it, someone else comes in and takes it from them!: "Hold on to what you have, so that no-one will take your crown" (Rev. 3:11). You're not yet out of the devil's firing line; "you have not yet resisted to the point of shedding your blood" (Heb. 12:4): let the kingdom always be before you, and resolutely believe in the things that are invisible. Don't let anything on this side of the other world get within you, and, above all, watch your own hearts carefully and the evil desires within them, for they are "deceitful above all things and beyond cure" (Jer. 17:9). Set your faces like flint; you have all power in heaven and earth on your side.'

Then Christian thanked him for his exhortation, but asked him, too, if he would tell them more things, to help them on the rest of the way, especially since they knew he was a prophet, and could tell them what might happen to them, and how they might resist and overcome difficulties. This request was supported by Faithful and so Evangelist began as follows:

'My sons, you've heard the true words of the gospel which say that "We must go through many hardships to enter the kingdom of God" (Acts 14:22), and again, that in "every city . . . prison and hardships" (Acts 20:23) face you. And therefore you can't expect to go very long on your pilgrimage without facing trouble of one sort or another. You've already seen something of the truth of these words and more will follow at once. As you can see, you're almost out of this wilderness, and you'll soon come into a town that you'll shortly see ahead of you. In that town you'll be heavily set upon by enemies, who will do their utmost to kill you. One or both of you must seal the testimony you hold with your blood. But, "Be faithful, even to the point of death, and I will give you the crown of life" (Rev. 2:10). Although his death will be unnatural, and his pain perhaps great, the one who dies there will still be better off than his companion, not only because he'll have arrived at the Celestial City sooner, but because he'll escape many miseries that the other will meet on the rest of his journey. When you've arrived at the town, and find that what I've said here is coming true, then remember your friend, quit yourselves like men, and "commit the keeping of your souls to God, as unto a faithful Creator".'

Then in my dream I saw that when they were out of the wilderness, they saw a town in front of them called Vanity. At this town there is a fair, called Vanity Fair, which keeps going all year long. It bears the name of Vanity Fair because the town is 'lighter than vanity', and also because all that is sold, and everything that comes there, is empty vanity, as the saying of the wise goes, 'everything is meaningless' (Eccles. 1:2, 14; 2:11, 17; 11:8; Isa. 40:17).

This fair is not newly-erected, but is a thing of ancient standing. I'll show you its origins. Almost five thousand years ago pilgrims were walking to the Celestial City, as these two honest men are. Beelzebub, Apollyon and Legion, with their companions, saw from the path that the pilgrims were following that their way to the city lay through this town of Vanity, and so they contrived to set up a fair here. It was to be a fair in which trash of all sorts would be sold, and it was to last all the year long. So at this fair many goods are on offer, such as houses, lands, jobs, places, honours, positions, titles, countries, kingdoms, evil desires, pleasures; and delights of all sorts, such as prostitutes, pimps, wives, husbands, children, masters, servants, lives, blood, bodies, souls, silver, gold, pearls, precious stones, and so on.

What's more, at all times you can see conjurers, tricksters, amusements, plays, fools, mimics, swindlers and hooligans of every kind. Here to be seen also, and that for nothing, are thefts, murders, adulteries and perjuries, blood-red in colour.

In other fairs on a lesser scale there are rows and streets, all called by their proper names, each selling different commodities, and here, in the same way, you have the proper places, the rows and streets (that is, countries and kingdoms) where the commodities of this fair can be quickly found. Here is the British row, the French row, the Italian row, the Spanish row, the German row, where different sorts of empty trivia are on sale. But, as in other fairs, one commodity in particular is given pride of place. Roman goods are promoted in this fair, and only our English nation, with a few others, have taken a dislike to this.

Now, as I said, the way to the Celestial City passes right through the town where this large fair is held. And anyone who wants to go to the city, and yet not go through this town, 'must needs go out of the world'. The Prince of princes himself, when he was here, went through this town to his own country, and that on a carnival day, too. I think it was Beelzebub, the chief lord of this fair, who invited him to buy some of his trash. Indeed he would have made him Lord of the fair, if only he had bowed down to Beelzebub as he went through the town. Because he was such a VIP Beelzebub took him from street to street, and quickly showed him all the kingdoms of the world to see if he could lure that Blessed One into cheapening himself by buying some of his trash. But he paid no attention to the merchandise and left the town without laying out so much as one penny (Matt. 4:8–9; Luke 4:5–7). So this fair is an ancient thing, of long standing, and a very great fair.

The Pilgrims enter the fair

Now these pilgrims, as I said, had to go through this fair, and so they did. But as they went into the fair, there was a commotion among all the people there and the whole town was in a hubbub about them. This happened for several reasons.

First, the pilgrims were wearing clothes that were quite different to any of the clothes on sale in the fair. So the people of the fair gaped at them. Some said they were fools, some that they were madmen, and some that they were outlandish foreigners (1 Cor. 4:9–10).

Second, their speech caused exactly the same bewilderment as their clothes, for few could understand what they said. These two naturally spoke the language of Canaan, but those who ran the fair were men of this world. From one end of the fair to the other Christian and Faithful were regarded as barbarians while the two pilgrims thought the same of the people of Vanity Fair.

Third, and this caused no small amusement to the stallholders, these pilgrims set little store by all their goods. They weren't interested even in looking at them. If the sellers called them to buy, they would put their fingers in their ears, and cry, 'Turn my eyes away from worthless things'; and they would look upwards, to show that their trade and traffic was in heaven (Ps. 119:37; Phil. 3:20–1).

One tried his luck. As he saw them pass by he called out mockingly, 'What will you buy?'

But they looked seriously at him, and said, 'We buy the truth' (Prov. 23:23).

This made everyone despise the men even more, some mocking, some taunting, some insulting and some calling on others to punch them. Finally things came to a head. There was such noise and chaos in the fair that all order was lost. Word was at once brought to the great one of the fair, who quickly came down. He deputed some of his most trusted friends to seize these men who had virtually turned the fair upside down and take them in for questioning. So the men were taken in, and their interrogators asked them where they came from, where they were going and what they were doing there in such strange garb. The men told them that

they were pilgrims and strangers in the world, and that they
were going to their own country, which was the heavenly
Jerusalem (Heb. 11:13–16). They said they'd not given the
townsmen or traders any cause to abuse them in this way,
and hinder them on their journey, except for one occasion,
when someone asked them what they wanted to buy, and
they said they wanted to buy the truth. But their interrogators thought they were lunatics and madmen, or else
troublemakers who had set out to disrupt the fair.

Christian and Faithful are put in a cage

So they took the two pilgrims and beat them. Then they
smeared them with filth, and put them in a cage as a spectacle for all the men of the fair. Christian and Faithful lay
there for some time, the objects of any man's sport, or
malice, or revenge, and the great one of the fair laughed at
all that happened to them. But the two men were patient,
"not repaying insult with insult, but with blessing" (1 Pet.
3:9), returning good words for bad, and kindness for
injuries. As a result, some men in the fair, who were more
observant and less prejudiced than the rest, restrained and
told off the baser sort for the abuses they continually meted
out to the two men. They however angrily let fly at these
others, reckoning them as bad as the men in the cage. They
accused these supporters of being in league with Christian
and Faithful and said they should be forced to suffer their
misfortune, too. The supporters replied that as far as they
could see the men were quiet and sober, and intended
nobody any harm. They went on to suggest that there were
many who traded in that fair who deserved the cage, and
the pillory, too, far more than these men whom they'd
abused.

After various words had passed on both sides (the two
prisoners consistently behaving very wisely and quietly in
front of them), they fell to fighting among themselves, and

injuring one another. So these two poor men were brought before their examiners once again, charged with being guilty of this latest disturbance in the fair. They were beaten pitilessly, irons were fastened on to them and they were led in chains up and down the fair, as an example and warning in case anybody else should speak up for them or join them. But Christian and Faithful behaved still more wisely. They received the humiliation and shame that were thrown at them with so much meekness and patience that several of the men of the fair were won over (though they were only few in comparison with the rest). This put the other side into an even greater rage, so much so that they decided the two men had got to die. They threatened that neither cage nor irons would be enough, but that they should die for the harm they'd done, and for deluding the men of the fair.

Christian and Faithful were remanded to the cage again until further orders could be given. They were put in the cage, and their feet were fastened in the stocks. However, they remembered what they'd heard from their faithful friend Evangelist. They were even more confirmed in their resolve to continue their present path and their sufferings by what he told them would happen to them. They now comforted each other, reminding each other that the one whose lot it was to suffer would have the best of it, and each man secretly wished that he might have that privilege. But committing themselves to the all-wise direction of the one who rules all things, they waited very contentedly as they were until other arrangements were made.

A date was fixed for their trial and condemnation and when the time came they were brought out before their enemies and charges were laid. Their judge's name was Lord Hategood. The content of their indictment was the same in each case, but the wording varied slightly. It said that they were enemies to, and disturbers of, their trade; that they had caused disturbances and divisions in the town; and had won a party to their own very dangerous opinions in contempt of the law of their prince.

Faithful began to answer. He said that he had only set himself against what had set itself against the One who is higher than the highest. And he added, 'As far as disturbing the peace goes, I've done nothing of the kind, because I'm a man of peace. The people who came over to us were won when they saw our truth and innocence, and they've only changed from the worse to the better. And as far as the king you talk of is concerned, since he's Beelzebub, the enemy of our Lord, I defy him and all his angels.'

Then a proclamation went out. It called for anyone who had anything to say for their lord and king against the prisoner at the bar to appear and give evidence. So three witnesses came – Envy, Superstition and Flatterer. They were asked if they knew the prisoner at the bar, and what they had to say for their lord the king against him.

Then Envy held forth. 'My lord, I've known this man a long time, and will attest upon my oath before this honourable bench that he is ...'

'Wait, administer the oath,' interrupted the Judge.

So they swore him in. Then he continued, 'My lord, this man, despite his plausible name, is one of the vilest men in our country. He respects neither prince nor people, law nor tradition, but does all that he can to spread his treacherous ideas, which he calls "principles of faith and holiness". In particular I myself once heard him affirm that Christianity and the customs of our town of Vanity are diametrically opposed, and can't be reconciled. In saying this, my lord, he at once not only condemns all our laudable activities, but us also for doing them.'

Then the Judge said, 'Have you anything more to say?'

'My lord, I could say much more, only I don't want to bore the court,' said Envy. 'Yet if need be, when the other gentlemen have given their evidence, rather than let anything be left out that could get rid of him, I'll give further evidence against him.'

So Envy was asked to stand down.

Next they called Superstition, and told him to look at the prisoner. They asked him what he could say for their lord the king against the prisoner and then swore him in.

Superstition began, 'My lord, I don't know this man very well, nor do I desire to. But I could tell from a conversation that I had with him in this town the other day that he's a thorough nuisance. I heard him say that our religion is worthless and we can't please God with it. And your lordship knows what that means. It means our worship gets us nowhere, we're still in our sins, and in the end we'll be damned. That's all I have to say.'

Then Flatterer was sworn in and invited to say what he knew on behalf of their lord the king against the prisoner at the bar.

'My lord, and all you gentlemen,' began Flatterer, 'I've known this fellow for a long time, and I've heard him say things that he ought not to have said. He's raged against our noble prince Beelzebub, and has spoken with contempt of his honourable friends, the Lord Oldman, the Lord Carnal-delight, the Lord Luxurious, the Lord Desire-of-Vain-glory, my old Lord Lechery, Sir Having Greedy, and all the rest of our nobility. What's more, he's said that if all men thought like him, possibly not one of these noble men would continue to exist in this town. Besides, he hasn't been afraid to rant and rave at you, my lord, you, who are appointed to be his judge, calling you an ungodly scoun-drel, and many other scandalous things. And he's smeared the characters of most of the dignitaries of our town in just the same way.'

When Flatterer had given his account, the Judge addressed the prisoner at the bar, 'You, deserter, heretic and traitor, have you heard what these honest gentlemen have testified against you?'

'May I speak a few words in my own defence?' asked Faithful.

The Judge replied, 'You, sir, don't deserve to live, you should die on the spot. But, so that everyone can see how kind we are, let's hear what you have to say – you vile deserter, you.'

Faithful's defence

Faithful spoke, 'In reply I say to Mr Envy that I've never said anything but this: any rule, or law, or custom, or people, that goes flatly against the word of God, is diametrically opposed to Christianity. If I've said anything wrong in saying this, convince me of my error and I'm willing in front of all of you to take my words back.

'As to the second charge, namely that from Mr Superstition, I only said that in the worship of God divine faith is required, but there can be no divine faith without a divine revelation of the will of God. So whatever is thrust into the worship of God that conflicts with divine revelation must have been from a man-made faith which will be of no benefit for eternal life.

'As to what Mr Flatterer said, putting on one side the accusation that I am said to rant and rave and so on, I say that the prince of this town, with all his attendant rabble named by this gentleman, are more fit for a place in hell than in this town and country, so the Lord have mercy upon me.'

Then the Judge called upon the jury who all this time were standing to hear and observe. 'Gentlemen of the jury,' he said, 'you see this man over whom there has been such a great uproar in this town. You have heard what these respectable gentlemen have witnessed against him, and you have also heard his reply and confession. It rests in your hands now to hang him, or save his life. Yet I think it right to instruct you in our law.

'An act was passed in the days of Pharaoh the Great, servant to our prince, to prevent adherents of an opposing religion increasing and growing too strong for him. This act laid down that their males should be thrown into the river

(Exod. 1). There was also a law passed in the days of Nebuchadnezzar the Great, another of his servants, which stated that whoever would not fall down and worship his golden image should be thrown into a fiery furnace (Dan. 3). Another law, made in the days of Darius, states that for a time whoever called upon any god but him should be cast into the lions' den (Dan. 6). Now the substance of these laws has been broken by this rebel, not only in thought, which is bad enough, but also in word and deed, which is quite intolerable.

'As far as Pharaoh's law goes, it was made to prevent mischief when that was just a possibility, and no crime was yet apparent. But here a crime is apparent, for you see in his second and third points he argues against our religion, and for the treason which he has openly confessed he deserves death.'

So the jury went out. Their names were Mr Blindman, Mr Nogood, Mr Malice, Mr Lovelust, Mr Liveloose, Mr Heady, Mr Highmind, Mr Enmity, Mr Liar, Mr Cruelty, Mr Hatelight and Mr Implacable. When they had talked together, each one gave in his personal verdict against the accused and then they unanimously voted to give the judge a verdict of guilty.

First Mr Blindman, the foreman, said, 'It's quite clear to me that this man is a heretic.'

Then Mr Nogood said, 'Rid the earth of such a fellow.'

'Ay,' said Mr Malice, 'I hate the very look of him.'

And Mr Lovelust said, 'I could never stand him.'

'Nor I,' said Mr Liveloose, 'he was for ever condemning my way of life.'

'Hang him, hang him,' said Mr Heady.

'A sorry sight,' said Mr Highmind.

'My heart rises up against him,' said Mr Enmity.

'He's a rogue,' said Mr Liar.

'Hanging's too good for him,' said Mr Cruelty.

'Let's do away with him,' said Mr Hatelight.

And then Mr Implacable said, 'Even if I were offered all

the world, I couldn't be reconciled to him. So let's at once pronounce him guilty of death.'

And so they did. Faithful was quickly condemned. He was to be returned to the place he'd been brought from and put to the most cruel death that could be invented.

The cruel death of Faithful

So they brought him out to deal with him according to their law. First they whipped him, then they beat him, then they lanced his flesh with knives. After that they stoned him, then pierced him with their swords, and finally they burned him to ashes at the stake. So it was that Faithful came to his end.

Now I saw that behind the crowds a chariot and two horses stood waiting for Faithful. As soon as his enemies had killed him, Faithful was taken up into the chariot. Immediately he was carried through the clouds and to the sound of the trumpet was taken by the nearest way to the Celestial Gate.

And for Christian there was some respite. He was sent back to prison where he remained for a while. But the One who overrules all things, and held all the power of their rage within his hands, enabled Christian to escape from them. So he went on his way, singing:

> Well, Faithful, thou hast faithfully profess'd
> Unto thy Lord, with whom thou shalt be bless'd,
> When *faithless* ones with all their vain delights,
> Are crying out under their hellish plights.
> Sing, Faithful, sing, and let thy name survive,
> For though they kill'd thee thou art yet alive.

14

Christian and Hopeful

Now I saw in my dream that Christian didn't go on alone. Someone whose name was Hopeful (this is what he became after observing the words and behaviour and all the suffering of Christian and Faithful at Vanity Fair) joined him as he walked. He made a brotherly pact with Christian and told him that he would be his companion. So one died to bear testimony to the truth, and another rose out of his ashes to be a companion for Christian on his pilgrimage. Hopeful also told Christian that many more of the men in the fair would, in their own time, follow after them.

Then I saw that very soon after leaving the fair they overtook someone ahead of them whose name was By-ends. They called to him, 'What town are you from, sir? And how far are you going along this path?'

He told them that he came from the town of Fairspeech, and was going to the Celestial City, but he didn't tell them his name.

'From Fairspeech!' said Christian. 'Is any good to be found there?' (Prov. 26:25).

'Yes,' said By-ends, 'I hope so.'

'Sir, what may I call you?' asked Christian.

'I'm a stranger to you and you to me,' By-ends said. 'If you're going this way, I'll be glad of your company, if not, I must rest content.'

'This town of Fairspeech, I've heard of it, and, as far as I remember, they say it's a wealthy place,' said Christian.

'Yes, I can assure you that it is and I've very many rich

relatives there.'

'Who are your relatives, if I may be so bold?' asked Christian.

'Almost the whole town, and in particular, my Lord Turnabout, my Lord Time-server, and my Lord Fairspeech, from whose ancestors that town first took its name. Also Mr Smoothman, Mr Facing-both-ways, Mr Anything; and the parson of our parish, Mr Two-tongues, who was my mother's own brother on my father's side. Well, to tell you the truth, I'm a gentleman of quality, yet my great grandfather was merely a boatman, looking one way and rowing another, and I got most of my wealth from the same occupation.'

'Are you a married man?' asked Christian.

'Yes. My wife is a very good woman, and the daughter of a good woman. She's my Lady Feigning's daughter, so she comes from a very distinguished family. She's so extremely refined that she knows how to take her refinement to everyone, from prince to pauper. It's true we differ slightly in our Christianity from those who are more religious, but only in two small points. First, we never struggle to swim against the wind and tide. Second, we are always most zealous when religion parades in his silver slippers. We do so love to walk with religion openly in the street if the sun shines, and the people applaud him.'

Then Christian moved a little aside to his companion Hopeful, and said, 'It crosses my mind that this chap is someone called By-ends, of Fairspeech, and if it is he we're in the company of as despicable a fellow as you'll find anywhere round here.'

Then Hopeful said, 'Ask him; I don't think he should be ashamed of his name.'

So Christian came up to him again and said, 'Sir, you talk as if you know something that the rest of the world doesn't know, and, if I don't miss my mark, I think I've half guessed who you are. Isn't your name Mr By-ends, of Fairspeech?'

'Certainly not! That's just a nickname given me by

people who can't stand me. And I must be willing to suffer this insult, as other good men have suffered insults before me.'

'But didn't you ever give anyone cause to call you this?' Christian asked.

How By-ends got his name

'Never! The worst I ever did to deserve it was that I always had the luck to judge the times and jump with the trend whatever it was, and do well for myself that way. But if things fall out that way, I'll count it a blessing. Why should malicious people load me with insults?' said By-ends.

'I thought you were the man I'd heard of,' Christian said. 'To tell you what I really think, I'm afraid this name applies to you more than you'd like us to think.'

'Well, if you like to think that, I can't help it. You'll find me good company if you'll still allow me to associate with you,' said By-ends.

'If you go with us,' Christian said, 'you must swim against the tide, which, I see, is contrary to your views. You must also own religion in his rags as well as in his silver slippers, and you must stand by him, too, when bound in irons, as well as when he walks the streets to cheers.'

'You must not impose your views, nor lord it over my faith. Leave me my liberty, and let me go with you,' said By-ends.

'Not a step farther, unless you accept what I've just said, and do as we do,' said Christian.

Then By-ends said, 'I'll never desert my old principles, since they're harmless and profitable. If I can't go with you, I must do as I did before you overtook me, and go by myself until someone overtakes me who'll be glad of my company.'

Now I saw in my dream that Christian and Hopeful left him, and kept their distance from him. But looking back one of them saw three men following Mr By-ends. As they came up to him he bowed very low and they complimented him. The men's names were Mr Hold-the-world, Mr Money-love, and Mr Saveall, men with whom Mr By-ends had formerly been acquainted. When they were young they were at school together, and were taught by a Mr Gripeman, a schoolmaster in Lovegain, which is a market-town in the county of Coveting, in the north. This schoolmaster taught them the art of getting, either by violence, deceit, flattery, lying, or by putting on a false religious front, and these four gentlemen had acquired so much from their master's art that they could each have run such a school themselves.

Well, as I said, when they'd greeted each other in this way, Mr Money-love said to Mr By-ends, 'Who is on the road ahead of us?' For Christian and Hopeful were still within sight.

'They're a couple of distant countrymen, who in their own way are off on a pilgrimage.'

'What a shame! Why didn't they stay? We might have had their good company. I hope we are all going on a pilgrimage,' said Money-love.

'We are indeed,' said By-ends. 'But the men in front of us are so puritanical and so fond of their own ideas, and think so little of the opinions of others, that be a man never so godly, if he doesn't go along with them in every detail, they throw him right out of their company.'

'That's bad,' said Saveall. 'But we read of people who are over-scrupulous and their rigidness makes them judge and condemn everyone but themselves. But what were the points you disagreed on?'

'Why in their headstrong way they've decided that it's their duty to rush on with their journey in all weathers, while I'm for waiting for wind and tide. They're for risking everything for God at once, in one go, and I'm for taking every opportunity to hold on to my life and possessions. They're for keeping to their ideas though all the world be against them, but I'm for religion as far as the times and my safety will bear it. They're for religion even in rags and in disgrace, but I'm for religion when he walks in his golden slippers, in the sunshine, to applause.'

Then Hold-the-world said, 'Yes, and stay as you are, good Mr By-ends. As far as I'm concerned, a man's a fool, who when he's free to keep what he has, is stupid enough to lose it. Let us be "wise as serpents"; it's best "to make hay when the sun shines"; you see how the bee lies still all winter, and stirs herself only when she can have profit accompanied by pleasure. God sometimes sends rain and sometimes sunshine. If they want to be stupid enough to go through the first, we'll be content to take fine weather along with us. For my part, I'd rather have a religion that promises us the security of God's good blessings. For what reasonable man could suppose that God, since he has bestowed on us all the good things of this life, wouldn't want us to keep them, for his sake? Abraham and Solomon grew rich in religion, and Job says that a good man "shall lay up gold as dust". He must not be like the men ahead of us, if they're as you've described them.'

'I think that we're all agreed about this, and so there's no need to waste any more words,' said Saveall.

Money-love agreed, 'No, there's certainly no need for any more words on this subject. For someone who believes neither Scripture nor reason – and you see we have both on our side – doesn't know his own freedom and doesn't seek his own safety.'

'My brothers,' said By-ends, 'as you see, we're going on a pilgrimage, and, to divert our minds from such negative things give me leave to put this question to you.

'Suppose a man, a minister or tradesman, or whoever, saw in front of him the opportunity of getting the good things of this life. But the only way he could do it was by – in appearance at least – becoming extraordinarily fervent about some aspects of religion that he'd had nothing to do with before. May he not use this means to attain his end, and still be a good honest man?'

Money-love replied, 'I see what you're getting at, and, with these gentlemen's kind permission, I'll try my best to give you an answer. First, with regard to your question concerning a *minister* himself. Suppose a minister, a worthy man, but with a very small living, has his eye on a greater one, far more fat and plump. And suppose he has the opportunity to get it, by being more studious, by preaching more frequently and fervently, and, because the nature of the congregation requires it, by altering some of his principles. For my part, I see no reason why a man may not do this, and remain an honest man, provided he has a call. Ay, and he may do a great deal more as well. And I'll tell you why:

'First, his desire for a better living is lawful – that can't be contradicted, as it's been set before him by Providence. So then he may try to get it if he can without disturbing his conscience.

'Second, his desire for that living makes him more studious, a more fervent preacher, and so on, and this makes him a better man. It makes him better and it improves his talents and this accords with the mind of God.

'Third, as for complying with the feelings of his people by denying some of his principles in order to serve them, this indicates, first that he is of a self-denying temperament, second that he has a sweet and winning way, and third that he is therefore more fit for the job of minister.

'Fourth, to conclude, a minister who changes a *small* for a *great* living should not be judged as covetous. Rather, since he has thereby become better qualified and more hard-working, he should be regarded as someone who pursues his calling and the opportunity given to him to do good.

'Which brings me to the second part of the question – concerning the *tradesman* you mentioned. Suppose such a person has only a poor business but by becoming religious can widen his market, perhaps get a rich wife, or more and superior customers for his shop. For my part, I see no reason why this may not be lawfully done. My reasons are:

'First, to become religious is a virtue, however it happens.

'Second, nor is it unlawful to marry a rich wife, or get more customers for my shop.

'Third, the man who gets these by becoming religious gets what is good, from those who are good, by becoming good himself. So then, here is a good wife, and good customers, and good profit, all by becoming religious, which is good. So, to become religious to gain all these things is a good and worthwhile policy.'

This answer by Mr Money-love to Mr By-ends' question, was much applauded by all of them, and they came to the conclusion that on the whole such a course of action was very advantageous. And because, as they thought, no one was able to contradict this argument and because Christian and Hopeful were still within calling distance, they enthusiastically agreed to attack them with this question as soon as they overtook them. They were especially keen since Christian and Hopeful had opposed Mr By-ends. So they called out to the two ahead of them who stopped and waited while they caught up. But as they approached they decided that not Mr By-ends, but old Mr Hold-the-world, should present the question. They thought an answer to him would be without any remaining heat that had been kindled between Mr By-ends and these two when they had parted earlier.

So they all met up, and after a brief greeting Mr Hold-the-world put the question to Christian and his friend, and invited them to answer it if they could.

So Christian replied, 'Even a babe in religion could answer thousands of such questions. For if it's not right to follow Christ for loaves of bread – as it's not (John 6:26) – how much more horrible is it to use him and religion as a cover to seize and enjoy the world? We find that only heathens, hypocrites, devils and witches, hold your opinion.

'First, heathens. For when Hamor and Shechem wanted

Jacob's daughter and cattle, and saw that the only way to get them was by being circumcised, they said to their companions, "If every male of us be circumcised, shall not their cattle, and their substance, and every beast of theirs be ours?" Their daughters and their cattle were what they were seeking, and their religion was the cover they made use of to achieve their ends. Read the whole story in Genesis 34:20–4.

'Second, the hypocritical Pharisees were also of this persuasion; they pretended to make long prayers, and intended to get widows' houses. Their judgment was greater damnation from God (Luke 20:46–7).

'Third, Judas the devil was the same. He was religious for the money bag (John 12:6), to get the contents for himself. As a result he was lost, cast away, and doomed to destruction (John 17:12).

'Fourth, Simon the magician held to this religion, too. He wanted to have the Holy Spirit to make money out of him, hence his sentence from Peter (Acts 8:18–23).

'Fifth, I can't help thinking that the man who takes up religion for the world, will throw away religion for the world. For just as surely as Judas became religious because he had designs on the world, so he also sold religion, and his Master, for the same reason.

'Therefore, to answer the question in the affirmative, as I see you've done, and to accept that as the true answer, is both un-Christian, hypocritical and devilish. And you'll get the reward your works deserve.'

Then they stood staring at one another, but weren't able to answer Christian. Hopeful also approved of the soundness of Christian's answer. So there was a great silence among them.

Mr By-ends and his company faltered and lagged behind, so that Christian and Hopeful might go ahead of them. Then Christian said to his companion, 'If these men can't stand before the sentence of men, what will they do with the sentence of God? And if they're dumb when dealt with by vessels of clay, what will they do when rebuked by the flames of a consuming fire?' (Exod. 24:17).

The danger of Lucre Hill

Then Christian and Hopeful went ahead of them again, and continued till they came to a pleasant plain called Ease, where they walked with great pleasure. But that plain was only narrow, so they were quickly over it. Now at the farther side was a small hill called Lucre, and in that hill there was a silver mine. Because of its rarity some of those who had previously passed that way had turned aside to see it. But they went too near the brink of the pit, where the ground was treacherous. It broke under their feet, and they were killed. Some had also been crippled there, and to their dying day couldn't be their own men again.

Then I saw in my dream that a little way off the road, close by the silver mine, Demas stood, looking like a very fine gentleman, and calling to passers-by to come and see. He said to Christian and his companion, 'Hi there! Come here, and I'll show you a thing or two.'

'What's so important that we've got to turn out of our way to see it?' asked Christian.

'It's a silver mine, with people digging in it for treasure. If you'll come you'll find that for only a little trouble you can set yourself up for life,' Demas said.

'Let's go and see,' said Hopeful.

'Not I,' said Christian. 'I've heard of this place, and of all the people that have been killed there. And, besides that, treasure always traps those who hunt for it. It stops them in their pilgrimage.'

Then Christian called to Demas, 'Isn't the place dangerous? Hasn't it hindered many in their pilgrimage?'

'Not very dangerous, unless you're careless.' But Demas blushed as he said this.

Then Christian said to Hopeful, 'Let's not stir a step out

of our way, but keep going.'

Hopeful added, 'I bet you that if By-ends receives the same invitation when he comes up, he'll turn aside to see.'

'No doubt of it – that's what his principles tell him to do – and a hundred to one he dies there.'

Then Demas called again, 'Won't you come over and see?'

But Christian answered roundly, 'Demas, you're an enemy to the Lord of this path, and to his ways. You've already been condemned by one of his Majesty's judges for turning aside yourself. Why are you trying to get us all condemned? (2 Tim. 4:10). Besides, if we turn aside, our Lord the King will certainly hear of it and instead of facing him boldly, we'll be in disgrace when we come before him.'

Demas protested that he was one of their fellowship too; and if they'd wait just a little he'd walk with them himself.

Then Christian said, 'What's your name? Isn't it what I've called you?'

'Yes, my name is Demas; I'm the son of Abraham.'

'I know you,' Christian said. 'Gehazi was your great-grandfather, and Judas your father, and you've followed their steps. It's nothing more nor less than a trick of the devil that you're using. Your father was hanged for a traitor, and you deserve no better (2 Kings 5:20–7; Matt. 26:14–15; 27:3–5). Rest assured that when we see the King we'll tell him of your conduct.' And so they went on their way.

By-ends goes over to Demas

By this time By-ends and his companions had again come within sight, and at his first signal they went over to Demas. Now, whether they fell into the pit as they looked over the brink, or whether they went down to dig, or whether they were smothered at the bottom by the damp fumes that frequently rise up, I'm not certain, but I did observe that they were never seen again on the way.

Then Christian sang:

> By-ends and silver Demas both agree;
> One calls, the other runs, that he may be
> A sharer in his lucre; so these two
> Take up in this world, and no further go.

Now just on the other side of this plain I saw the pilgrims came to a place where an old monument was standing close by the roadside. They stopped, worried by the strangeness of its shape, for it looked as if it had been a *woman* transformed into a pillar. They stood staring and staring at it, but for some time couldn't think what to make of it. At last Hopeful spotted something written on the top. It was in an unusual script and, being no scholar, he called to Christian, who was an educated man, to see if he could pick out the meaning. So Christian came and, after spending a little while working out the letters, he found that it read: 'Remember Lot's wife'. He read it to his companion and they both decided that that was the pillar of salt into which Lot's wife was turned for looking back greedily when she was escaping from Sodom (Gen. 19:26). This sudden and amazing sight led to the following conversation.

'Well, brother!' Christian said. 'This comes as a timely warning after Demas's invitation to come over and look at Lucre Hill. Had we done as he wanted – and as you were inclined to do – for all I know we ourselves might have been turned into a spectacle, like this woman, for everyone who comes after to stare at.'

'I'm sorry I was so foolish,' Hopeful said. 'It's a wonder the same thing didn't happen to me. What's the difference between her sin and mine? She only looked back, and I wanted to go and see. Praise God for his grace to me! I'm ashamed of what was in my heart.'

'Let's take careful note of what we see here so that it will help us in the future,' Christian said. 'This woman escaped one judgment – she didn't fall when Sodom was destroyed. Yet she was destroyed by a second judgment. So here she is, turned into a pillar of salt.'

'True,' added Hopeful, 'she can be both a warning and an example to us. A warning to us to steer clear of her sin, and an example of the judgment that'll overtake any who aren't put off by this warning. So Korah, Dathan, and Abiram, with the 250 men who perished in their sin, were a lesson and an example to others (Num. 26:9–10). I wonder how Demas and his companions can stand so confidently over there looking for that treasure when this woman was turned into a pillar of salt, just for looking behind her – for we don't read that she put as much as a foot out of the way – especially as the pillar is within sight of where they are. They're bound to see her, if they'd only lift up their eyes.'

'It does make you wonder,' Christian agreed. 'And it shows how desperate they are. They're like nothing so much as thieves who pick pockets in the presence of the judge, or steal purses under the gallows. It's said of the men of Sodom that they were wicked because they were sinning greatly against the Lord (Gen. 13:13), that is, in his presence, and in spite of the kindness that he'd showed them, for the land of Sodom was like the Garden of Eden in earlier times (Gen. 13:10). This made him more angry and made their plague as hot as the Lord's fire out of heaven could make it. It follows that others like them – including these men there – who sin in his sight, right in the face of examples warning them to the contrary, must experience the severest of judgments.'

'I'm sure that's true,' said Hopeful, 'but what a mercy it is that neither you nor I, especially I, have let ourselves become such an example! This gives us cause to thank God, to fear him, and always to remember Lot's wife.'

15

Doubting Castle and Giant Despair

A river

I saw then that they went on their way to a pleasant river, which David the king called 'the river of God', but John, 'the river of the water of life' (Ps. 46:4; 65:9; Ezek. 47:1–9; Rev. 22:1). Now their way lay along the bank of the river, and here Christian and his companion walked with great delight. They also drank the water from the river, which was pleasant and refreshed their weary spirits. On each side of the river banks there were green trees bearing many kinds of fruit, the leaves of which were good for medicine. They were delighted with the fruit and they ate the leaves to cure over-eating and other illnesses which come to people who get overheated through travelling. On either side of the river there was a meadow, where beautiful and rare lilies grew, and it was green all the year long. In this meadow they lay down and slept, for here they were quite safe. (Ps. 23:2; Isa. 14:30). When they woke they again picked fruit from the trees, and drank the water and then lay down to sleep. In this way several days and nights went by. Then they sang:

Behold ye how these crystal streams do glide,
To comfort pilgrims by the highway-side.
The meadows green, besides their fragrant smell,
Yield dainties for them; and he that can tell
What pleasant fruit, yea, leaves, these trees do yield,
Will soon sell all that he may buy this field.

When they were ready to go on – for they were not yet at the end of their journey – they ate and drank, and then left.

Now I saw in my dream that they had not travelled far before the river and the path diverged for a while. They were not a little sorry to see this, yet they dared not leave the path. Now the path from the river was rough, and their feet were tender as a result of their travels. The pilgrims felt discouraged because of the path (Num. 21:4), and wished it were better. Now not far in front of them, on the left-hand side of the road, there was a meadow, called By-path meadow, and a stile leading into it.

Then Christian said to his companion, 'If this meadow lies alongside our path, let's go over into it.'

He went to the stile to see, and sure enough, a path ran parallel to theirs on the other side of the fence.

'Just what I was wanting,' Christian said. 'The going will be easier here. Come on, Hopeful, let's go over.'

'But what if this path should lead us out of the way?' Hopeful asked.

'That isn't very likely,' said his friend. 'Look, it runs along by the side of ours.'

So Hopeful, having been persuaded by his companion, went after him over the stile, and together they set off along the path in the field, finding it very easy to walk on. Then, looking ahead, they spotted a man walking as they did (his name was Vain-Confidence). So they called out to him, and asked him where the path led.

'To the Celestial Gate,' he said.

'Look,' said Christian, 'didn't I tell you? That shows we're right.'

So they followed, while he went ahead of them. But night came on, and it grew very dark, so that those behind lost sight of the man in front.

Then Vain-Confidence, who couldn't see the path now, fell into a deep pit (Isa. 9:16), which had been purposely dug there by the prince of those grounds in order to catch overconfident fools. And Vain-Confidence was dashed in pieces by his fall.

Christian and his companion heard the sound of falling and called out to know what was the matter. But there was no answer, only a groaning.

Then Hopeful said, 'Where are we now?'

But Christian was silent, suddenly afraid that he'd led them out of the way. And now it began to rain and thunder, and lightning began to flash in a dreadful way. And the water rose violently.

Then Hopeful groaned and said, 'Oh, if only I'd kept on my path!'

Christian said, 'Who'd have thought that this path would have led us out of the way?'

'From the beginning I was afraid of this,' said Hopeful. 'That's why I gave you that gentle warning. I'd have spoken more plainly, except that you're older than I.'

'Good brother, don't be angry with me. I'm sorry I've led you out of the way, and have brought you into such danger. Please, forgive me, I didn't intend any harm.'

'Don't be upset, brother. I forgive you, and what's more, I believe that this will work out for our good.'

'I am glad I'm with a Christian brother who's so forgiving. But we mustn't stand about. Let's try to go back again.'

'But, good brother, let me go on ahead.'

'No, if you don't mind, let me go first, so that if there is any danger I may be the first to face it, because it's all my fault that we've both left the path.'

'No,' said Hopeful, 'you mustn't go first. You're too upset and may lead us out of the way again.'

Then, to encourage them, they heard a voice saying, 'Take note of the highway, the road that you take. Return . . .' (Jer. 31:21).

By this time the water was very high, so that the way back was dangerous. (As I watched I thought that it's easier going out of the way when we're in it, than going in when we're out.) But they risked the return journey though the night was so dark, and the flood so high that nine or ten times they were on the verge of drowning.

Christian and Hopeful sleep in the grounds of Giant Despair

For all their skill, they couldn't make it to the stile that night, so coming at last across a small shelter, they sat down to wait till daybreak. However, overcome by tiredness, they fell asleep.

Now not far from where they were lying there was a castle. It was called Doubting Castle and was owned by Giant Despair and it was in his grounds they were now sleeping. The next morning he got up early and as he was walking up and down in his fields, he caught Christian and Hopeful asleep in his grounds. Grimly he ordered them to wake up and angrily asked where they were from, and what they were doing in his grounds. They told him they were pilgrims and that they had lost their way.

Then the Giant said, 'Last night you trespassed on my property, you trampled on my ground and lay down on it, and therefore you must come along with me.'

So they were forced to go because he was stronger than they were. Also there was nothing they could say, for they knew they were in the wrong. So the Giant drove them in front of him to his castle and threw them into a very dark, nasty and stinking dungeon. Here then they lay from Wednesday morning till Saturday night, without one bit of bread, or one drop of drink. There was no light, and no one to ask how they were. Now their plight was evil indeed for they were far from friends and acquaintances (Ps. 88:18). And in this place Christian's sorrow was doubled because it was through his ill-advised counsel that they had come into this misery.

Now Giant Despair had a wife, and her name was Diffidence. When he was gone to bed he told his wife what he'd done. He said he had taken a couple of prisoners and cast them into his dungeon for trespassing on his grounds. And he asked her what else it would be best to do to them. She asked who they were, where they had come from and where they were bound for, and he told her. Then she advised him that when he got up in the morning he should beat them mercilessly.

So when he got up he armed himself with a deadly crab-tree cudgel, and went down into the dungeon. First he set about berating his prisoners as if they were dogs, although they never uttered one angry word. Then he fell upon them and beat them fearfully, till they were helpless, unable even to turn over on the floor. This done he withdrew, leaving them there to grieve in their misery, and suffer in their distress. All that day passed in sighs and bitter lamentations.

The next night Diffidence again talked with her husband about Christian and Hopeful and hearing that they were still alive, she said, 'Advise them to do away with themselves.'

So when morning came he went to them again, behaving as disagreeably as ever. Seeing that they were very sore from the beating that he'd given them the day before, he told them that since they were never likely to come out of that place the only thing to do was to make an end of themselves at once, either with a knife, by a noose, or poison.

'Why,' he said, 'should you choose life, since it brings so much bitterness?'

But they asked him to let them go.

With that he glared furiously at them and rushing to them would without doubt have finished them off himself, but he fell into one of his fits (for in the hot sun he sometimes had fits, and for a time lost the use of his hands). So he came away, leaving them as before to consider what to do. Then the prisoners talked together about whether or not it was better to take his advice.

'Brother,' Christian said, 'what shall we do? Our life is wretched now. For my part, I don't know whether it's better to live like this, or die out of hand. "I prefer strangling and death, rather than this body of mine" (Job 7:15), and the grave would be more comfortable than this dungeon. Shall we do what the giant says?'

'It's true that our present condition is dreadful, and I find death far more welcome than living like this for ever,' Hopeful said. 'But let's think about it. The Lord of the country to which we're going has said, "You shall not murder." We're forbidden to kill another human being, so how much more are we forbidden to follow the giant's advice and kill ourselves? Besides, to kill another person is merely killing a body but to kill oneself is to kill body and soul at once. And moreover, my brother, you talk of comfort in the grave, but have you forgotten the hell to which murderers certainly go? For "no murderer has eternal life in him" (1 John 3:15). And let's consider again that Giant Despair hasn't taken all the power of the law into his own hands. Others, as far as I can understand, have been captured by him as well, and yet have escaped out of his hands. Who knows but that God, who made the world, may cause that Giant Despair to die? At some time or other he may forget to lock us in, or maybe he'll soon have another of his fits in front of us, and lose the use of his limbs. If that should ever happen again, I'm resolved to act like a man and try my utmost to get away. I was a fool not to try before. But come what may, brother, let's be patient and endure it a while. Time may give us a happy release. Don't let's be our own murderers.'

With these words Hopeful restrained his brother. So that day passed, with the two prisoners lying miserably together in the dark.

Towards evening the Giant went down into the dungeon again to see if his prisoners had followed his advice. He found them alive, but that was all you could say. What with the lack of bread and water, and with the wounds they had received when he beat them, they could do little but breathe. But, as I say, he found them alive, and at this he fell into a furious rage, and told them that since they had disobeyed his counsel it would be worse for them than if they'd never been born.

At this they trembled violently, and I think that Christian fainted. When he had recovered slightly, they renewed their conversation about the Giant's advice, and discussed whether or not they had better take it. Now Christian again seemed to be for doing away with themselves, but Hopeful replied a second time as follows.

'My brother,' he said, 'don't you remember how brave you've been up to how? Apollyon couldn't crush you, nor could anything that you heard or saw or felt in the Valley of the Shadow of Death. Think what hardship, terror, and bewilderment you've already gone through, and after all that are you reduced to a bundle of fears? I'm in the dungeon with you, and I'm a far weaker man by nature than you are. This giant has wounded me as well as you, and has cut off my supply of bread and water, and like you I pine for the light. But let's just exercise a little more patience. Remember how brave you were at Vanity Fair, and how you were neither afraid of the chain nor the cage, nor even of bloody death. So let us bear up with patience as well as we can, even if only to avoid the shame that it ill becomes a Christian to be found in.'

Now it was night again, and when the Giant and his wife were in bed she asked him about the prisoners, and whether they had taken his advice. He replied, 'They're stubborn rogues, they'd rather bear any hardship then do away with themselves.'

Then she said, 'Tomorrow, take them into the castle-yard, and show them the bones and skulls of those you've already dispatched, and make them believe that before the end of the week you'll tear them to pieces, as you've done to their like before them.'

So when morning came the Giant went to them again, and taking them into the castle-yard he showed them the bones, as his wife had suggested. 'These,' he said, 'were once pilgrims, as you are. They trespassed on my grounds,

as you've done, and when I was ready I tore them to pieces,
and within ten days I'll do the same to you. Be off! Get
down to your cell again.' And with that he beat them all the
way there. So all Saturday they lay there in a terrible state,
as before.

Now when it was night and when Mrs Diffidence and her
husband the Giant were in bed, they began to talk again
about their prisoners. The Giant was surprised that neither
his blows nor his advice could finish them off.

His wife replied, 'I'm afraid they're living in the hope
that someone will come to set them free. Or they've
picklocks on them, and hope to escape that way.'

'Do you think so, my dear?' the Giant said. 'I'll search
them in the morning.'

Well, about midnight on Saturday Christian and Hopeful
began to pray, and continued in prayer till almost daybreak.

A key called Promise opens any lock in Doubting Castle

A little before it was day Christian, now half beside himself,
broke out passionately, 'What a fool I am lying like this in a
stinking dungeon when I could be free. I've a key in my
breast called Promise and I'm certain it'll open any lock in
Doubting Castle.'

Then Hopeful said, 'That's good news, brother, get it out
and try.'

Christian pulled it out and tried it at the dungeon door.
As he turned the key the lock was released and the door
swung open. So Christian and Hopeful both came out.
Then Christian went to the outer door that leads into the
castle-yard, and the key opened that door, too. After that
he went to the iron gate, which also had to be opened. That
lock was desperately hard, yet the key eventually turned.
They pushed open the gate and quickly escaped. But as it
opened that gate creaked so loudly that Giant Despair

woke up. He jumped up hastily out of bed to chase his prisoners but felt his limbs go weak as his fits seized him again. So he was unable to go after them.

Christian and Hopeful went on till they came to the King's highway again and there they were safe because they were out of the Giant's jurisdiction.

A pillar erected by Christian and Hopeful

When they had climbed over the stile they discussed what they could do to stop others who came after from falling into the hands of Giant Despair. After a while they agreed to erect a pillar at the stile, and to engrave this sentence on its side, 'Over this stile lies the way to Doubting Castle, which is kept by Giant Despair. He despises the King of the Celestial Country, and seeks to destroy his holy pilgrims.' Many who followed after them read what was written, and escaped danger.

This done, they sang,

Out of the way we went, and then we found
What 'twas to tread upon forbidden ground:
And let them that come after have a care,
Lest heedlessness makes them as we to fare;
Lest they, for trespassing, his prisoners are,
Whose Castle's Doubting, and whose name's Despair.

16

The Delectable Mountains

Then they went on till they came to the Delectable Mountains which belong to the Lord of the hill of which we spoke earlier. Christian and Hopeful went up the mountains to see the gardens and orchards, the vineyards and fountains. Here they were able to drink and wash themselves, and they were free to eat as much fruit as they wanted from the vineyards. Now shepherds were feeding their flocks on the higher slopes of these mountains, and they were standing by the side of the road. The pilgrims therefore went to them and, leaning upon their sticks as weary pilgrims do when they stand to talk with anyone by the way, they asked, 'Whose Delectable Mountains are these? And who do the sheep belong to?'

The shepherds said, 'These mountains are part of Emmanuel's Land, and they're within sight of his city. The sheep are also his, and he laid down his life for them' (John 10:11).

'Is this the way to the Celestial City?' asked Christian.

'You're on the right path,' they replied.

'How far is it?'

'Too far for anyone, except those who are bound to get there.'

'Is the path safe or dangerous?'

'Safe for those for whom it is meant to be safe, "but the rebellious stumble in them"' (Hos. 14:9).

'Can pilgrims who are weary and faint with the journey find somewhere to rest in this place?'

'The Lord of these mountains commanded us: "Do not forget to entertain strangers" (Heb. 13:2). Therefore the hospitality of our land is open to you,' the shepherds replied.

The Shepherds welcome Christian and Hopeful

I also saw in my dream that when the shepherds realised that Christian and Hopeful were travellers they asked them questions which they answered in their usual way. So they were asked, 'Where are you from?' and 'How did you get on to the way?' and 'How have you managed to keep going?' For very few of those who set out are seen on these mountains. When the shepherds heard their answers they were very pleased, and looked at them with love.

'Welcome to the Delectable Mountains,' they said.

The Mountain of Error

The shepherds, whose names were Knowledge, Experience, Watchful and Sincere, took their hands and led them to their tents, urging them to eat and drink. They also said, 'We wish you would stay here awhile, to get to know us, and to refresh yourselves with all the good things of these Delectable Mountains.'

Christian and Hopeful told the shepherds that they were very happy to stay. And so they went to rest, because it was very late.

Then in my dream I saw that in the morning the shepherds invited Christian and Hopeful to walk with them in the mountains. So they went out, and walked for a while, admiring the views on every side.

Then the Shepherds said to each other, 'Shall we show these pilgrims some amazing things?' When they had agreed, they led them first to the top of a hill called Error, which was very steep on the farther side, and told them look down. So Christian and Hopeful looked down and at the bottom they saw the bodies of several men, dashed to pieces as a result of falling from the top.

Then Christian said, 'What does this mean?'

The shepherds answered, 'Haven't you heard of the people who went astray through listening to Hymenaeus and Philetus talking about the resurrection of the body?' (2 Tim. 2:17–18).

'Yes,' they said.

Then the shepherds said, 'Those are the same men. Those are their bodies, dashed to pieces at the bottom of this mountain. They've remained unburied there to this day, as you see, as a warning to others to be careful in case they clamber too high, or come too near the brink of this mountain.'

Mount Caution

Then I saw that they were taken to the top of another mountain, called Caution, and told to look in the distance. When they did they thought they saw several men walking up and down among the tombs that were there. The men seemed to be blind, because they sometimes stumbled over the tombs, and couldn't find their way out.

Then Christian said, 'What does this mean?'

The shepherds answered, 'Just before coming to these mountains, didn't you see a stile leading into a meadow on the left-hand side of this path?'

'Yes,' they answered.

Then the shepherds said, 'From that stile a path leads straight to Doubting Castle, which is owned by Giant Despair. These men were pilgrims, as you are now, till they came to that stile. And because the right path was rough just there, they chose to go out of it into the meadow. But there they were captured by Giant Despair, and cast into

Doubting Castle. After holding them for a while in the dungeon, he eventually put out their eyes. Then he led them among those tombs, where he's left them to wander to this very day so that the saying of the wise man might be fulfilled: "A man who strays from the path of understanding comes to rest in the company of the dead"' (Prov. 21:16).

Christian and Hopeful looked at each other with tears running down their cheeks, but said nothing to the shepherds.

Then in my dream I saw the shepherds take them to a deep abyss, where there was a door in the side of the hill. Opening the door, they told Christian and Hopeful to look in. Inside it was very dark and smoky. The pilgrims thought they heard a rumbling noise, like a fire, and a cry as if someone was tormented, and they smelt sulphur.

Then Christian said, 'What does this mean?'

The shepherds told them, 'This is a side-road to hell. It's the way that hypocrites enter – the sort who sell their birthright, with Esau; and sell their Master, with Judas; the sort who blaspheme the gospel, with Alexander; and lie and deceive, with Ananias and Sapphira, his wife.'

Then Hopeful said to the shepherds, 'Didn't each one of these men have the mark of a pilgrim as we have now?'

'Yes, and held it a long time, too.'

'How far did they travel on their pilgrimage before being so miserably cast away?'

'Some farther, and some not so far as these mountains,' said the shepherds.

Then the pilgrims said to each other, 'We need to cry to the Strong One for strength!'

'Yes – and you'll have need of it when you get it, too.'

By this time the pilgrims were keen to move on and the shepherds felt the same, so they walked together towards the end of the mountains.

Then the shepherds said to each other, 'If the pilgrims have the skill to look through our telescope let's show them the gates of the Celestial City.'

Christian and Hopeful lovingly accepted this suggestion. So the shepherds led them to the top of a high hill, called Clear, and gave them the telescope to look through.

They tried to look, but the memory of that last sight made their hands shake, and as a result they couldn't look steadily through the glass. Yet they thought they saw something like the gate, and also some of the glory of the place. Then they went away, singing this song:

> Thus by the shepherds secrets are reveal'd,
> Which from all other men are kept conceal'd.
> Come to the shepherds, then, if you would see
> Things deep, things hid, and that mysterious be.

When they were about to leave one of the shepherds gave them a note about the way; another bade them beware of the flatterer; a third told them to be careful not to sleep on the enchanted ground; and a fourth bade them Godspeed. So I woke up from my dream.

17

The Enchanted Ground, and the descent to it

I slept, and dreamed again, and saw the same two pilgrims
going down the mountains, along the highway towards the
city. Now a little below these mountains, on the left-hand
side, lies the country of Conceit. A little crooked lane leads
from this country and joins the path along which the pilgrims
were walking. Here they met a very lively young man who
came from that country, and whose name was Ignorance.
Christian asked him where he had come from and where he
was going.

Ignorance said, 'Sir, I was born in the country that lies
over there to our left, and I'm going to the Celestial City.'

'But how do you think you'll get in at the gate? You may
encounter some difficulty there,' Christian said.

'As other good people do,' he replied.

'But what do you have to show at the gate, to cause it to be
opened for you?'

'I know my Lord's will, and have lived a good life. I pay
every man what I owe him. I pray, fast, pay tithes, and give
to charity, and have left my country for the one I'm going to.'

'But you didn't come in at the wicket-gate at the head of
this path. You came in along that winding lane, and therefore
I'm afraid that no matter what you think you're entitled to,
when the day of reckoning comes you'll be accused of being a
thief and a robber, instead of being admitted into the city.'

'Gentlemen, you're utter strangers to me. I don't know
you. Just you follow the religion of your country, and I'll follow mine. And I hope everything will turn out all right. As for

the gate that you talk of, all the world knows that it's a long way off from our country. I can't think of a man in our parts who even knows the way to it, and it doesn't matter, anyway, since as you see we have a fine, pleasant, green lane that comes down from our country, and is the nearest way into the path.'

When Christian saw that the man was convinced that his own opinion was right, he whispered to Hopeful, '"There is more hope for a fool than for him"' (Prov. 26:12); and added, '"Even as he walks along the road, the fool lacks sense and shows everyone how stupid he is" (Eccles. 10:3). What do you think?' Christian asked Hopeful. 'Shall we carry on talking to him or go ahead for the time being, and leave him to think over what he's already heard? We can stop for him later on and see if bit by bit we can do him any good.'

Then Hopeful said:

> Let Ignorance a little while now muse
> On what is said, and let him not refuse
> Good counsel to embrace, lest he remain
> Still ignorant of what's the chiefest gain.
> God saith, those that no understanding have,
> Although he made them, them he will not save.

Hopeful added, 'I don't think it'll do any good to tell him everything all at once. Let's pass on ahead, as you suggest. We'll talk to him again later and tell him as much as he can take in.'

So they both went on, and Ignorance followed. Now when they had gone on a little way they entered a very dark lane where they met a man whom seven devils had bound with seven strong cords. Now they were carrying him back to a door in the side of the hill (Matt. 12:45; Prov. 5:22). When he saw this, Christian began to tremble, and so did Hopeful. As the devils led the man away, Christian looked to see if he knew him, and he thought it might be a man called Turnaway, who lived in the town of Apostasy. But Christian didn't get a good view of the man's face, for he hung his head like a thief caught redhanded. When he had gone past Hopeful looked after him and saw on his back a paper with this inscription: 'Shameless believer and damnable apostate.'

Then Christian said to his companion, 'This reminds me of something that I've been told happened to a good man around here. His name was Little-faith, but he was a good man, and he lived in the town of Sincere. It was this. At the entrance to this passage a lane comes down from Broadway-gate called Deadman's-lane because of the murders that are frequently committed there. And this Little-faith, who was going on pilgrimage like us, chanced to sit down there and sleep.

'Now it so happened that just then three hooligans came down the lane from Broadway-gate. They were three brothers, and their names were Faint-heart, Mistrust, and Guilt. Catching sight of Little-faith they came galloping up. Now he had just woken up from his sleep and was getting ready to continue his journey. So they all came up to him, and with threatening language told him to stand still. At this Little-faith looked as white as a sheet, and was powerless to fight or fly. Then Faint-heart said, 'Hand over your purse.'

'But when he was slow to move (for he was loth to lose his money), Mistrust ran up to him and pushing his hand into his pocket pulled out a bag of silver.

'Then Little-faith cried out, "Thieves, thieves!"

'At that Guilt struck Little-faith on the head with the great club that he was holding and felled him to the ground, where he lay bleeding as if he'd bleed to death. All this time the thieves were hanging about, but at last, hearing someone on the road, and fearing that it might be Great-grace, who lives in the town of Goodconfidence, they took to their heels, and left this good man to shift for himself. Eventually Little-faith came to, and getting up, attempted to struggle on his way. This was the story.'

'But did they take everything he possessed?' Hopeful asked.

'No,' Christian replied, 'They didn't search the place where his jewels were hidden. So he still had those. But I was told that he was very upset by his loss because the thieves had got most of his spending money. As I said, he was left with his jewels, and he also had some small change left, but scarce enough to take him to his journey's end (1 Pet. 4:18). In fact, if what I've heard is true, he was forced to beg as he went to keep himself alive, for he couldn't sell his jewels. But beg and do as he might, he went with an empty stomach for much of the rest of the way.'

'But what a wonder that they didn't take the certificate that he needed to gain admission at the Celestial Gate!'

'It is a wonder. But they didn't get it – though it was no thanks to him that they missed it. He was so petrified when they came at him that it was beyond him to hide anything. So it was more by good providence than by his own efforts that they missed it' (2 Tim. 1:14; 2 Pet. 2:9).

'But it must have been a comfort to him that they didn't get his jewels.'

'It might have been a great comfort had he let it be. But those who told me the story said that he drew little comfort from it all the rest of the way because of his dismay at the loss of his money. Indeed, he forgot about it for most of the time. On top of that, whenever it came into his mind, and he began to be comforted, fresh thoughts of his loss would surge into his mind again and swallow up everything else.'

'Alas, poor man! He must have been devastated.'

'You can say that again! Which of us wouldn't have felt the same, if we'd been robbed and injured, too, and in a strange place, as he was? It's a wonder he didn't die of grief, poor fellow! I was told that he scattered nothing but bitter, mournful complaints along almost all the rest of the route. He told the whole story to everyone who overtook him, or whom he overtook – where he was robbed and how, who did it and what he'd lost, and how he'd been wounded and hardly escaped with his life.'

'But it's a wonder that he wasn't forced to sell or pawn some of his jewels so that he might have the wherewithal to relieve his suffering on his journey,' Hopeful said.

'You're talking as if you're still not out of your shell! What could he pawn them for? Who could he sell them to? People thought nothing of his jewels in the land where he was robbed. Anyway, he didn't want comfort at the cost of losing his jewels. And had they been missing when he reached the gate of the Celestial City, he would have been cut off from his inheritance there. He knew that well enough and that would have been worse than the sight of ten thousand thieves or any villainy they could practise.'

'Why're you so prickly all of a sudden? Esau sold his birthright for a bowl of stew, and that birthright was his greatest jewel (Heb. 12:16). So why couldn't Little-faith do the same?'

'Esau did sell his birthright, that's true,' Christian said, 'and so do many others, as well, and by doing that they exclude themselves from the greatest blessing, as that poor fool did. But you must distinguish between Esau and Little-faith, and between their possessions. Esau's birthright was typical of man in general, but Little-faith's jewels were not. Esau's stomach was his god, but Little-faith's stomach was not. Esau's weakness lay in his physical appetites, but Little-faith's did not. Esau could see no farther than the satisfaction of his lusts. "Look, I am about to die," he said, "What good is the birthright to me?" (Gen. 25:32). But Little-faith, though it was his lot to have only a *little* faith, was kept by his little faith from such extremes and enabled to see his jewels for what they were and prize them too much to sell them, as Esau did his birthright. You don't read anywhere that Esau had faith, not even a *little* faith. It's not surprising that where the flesh rules supreme (as it does in someone who has no faith to resist it) a man will sell his birthright, and his soul, and everything, even to the devil in hell. People like that are like the wild donkey, "Who in her heat cannot be restrained" (Jer. 2:24). When their minds are set upon their lusts, they will have them, whatever the cost. But Little-faith was different. His mind was on divine things, his way of life was based upon things that were spiritual and from above. Therefore what was the point of selling his jewels – even supposing there'd been someone to buy them – in order to fill his mind with empty rubbish? Will a man pay to fill his stomach with hay? Or can you persuade the turtle-dove to live upon carrion like the crow? Though people without faith who want to satisfy their physical passions will pawn, or mortgage, or sell what they have, and themselves into the bargain, yet anyone who has faith – saving faith – even though it's very small, just can't do that. This, brother, is where your mistake lies.'

'I admit it. But your sharp retort almost made me angry.'

'Why? I only compared you to a lively bird who runs backwards and forwards on footpaths with its shell still on its head. But let it be. Let's return to the subject under discussion, and everything will be all right between us.'

'But, Christian, I'm convinced that these three fellows were just a bunch of cowards. Why else did they run off when they heard someone coming along the road? Why didn't Little-faith pluck up a bit of courage? It seems to me he could have had one brush with them and then given in when there was no help for it.'

'They are cowards – many have said that – but not many have tried to prove it when put to the test. As for courage, Little-faith had none. And what about you? You were for having one brush with them, and then giving in. Since this is all your stomach can take when they're at a distance from us, if they should appear in front of you, as they did to him, they might make you think again.

'And besides,' continued Christian, 'think about this. Those thieves are just mercenaries. They serve under the king of the bottomless pit, who, if need be, will come to their aid himself, and his voice is like the roaring of a lion (1 Pet. 5:8). I myself have been confronted, as Little-faith was. And it was terrible. These three villains set upon me, and I was beginning to resist like a Christian, when they just called out, and in came their master. I was a goner, except that I was wearing first-rate armour. Even so, I found it hard work to face up to them. No one can describe what you go through in that combat except someone who's been in the battle himself.'

'Yes,' agreed Hopeful, 'but you see they did run away when they only thought that Great-grace was coming.'

The King's champions

'True. Often Great-grace has only had to appear and they've fled – they and their master. And no wonder, for he's the King's champion. But I presume you'll grant that there's some difference between Little-faith and the King's champion. Not all the King's subjects are his champions, nor, when put to the test, are they able to perform the sort of feats he can do. Is it right to think that a little child should handle Goliath as David did? Or that a wren should have an ox's strength? Some are strong, some are weak; some have great faith, some have little. This man was one of the weak, and therefore he went to the wall.'

'I wish for their sakes that it had been Great-grace.'

'If it had been, he might have had his hands full. I must tell you that though Great-grace is a skilled swordsman, and has done very well against them, and will do again, as long as he keeps them at sword's point, if they get within his guard – even men like Faint-heart, Mistrust, or the other – it'll still be a hard fight, but they'll end up throwing him. And you know, when a man is down, what can he do? If you look carefully at Great-grace's face, you'll see scars and cuts there that prove what I say. Indeed, once I heard that when he was in such combat he said, "We despaired even of life" (2 Cor. 1:8). Remember how these violent ruffians and their companions made David groan, despair and cry out! Heman and Hezekiah too, though they were champions in their day, were forced to stir themselves when attacked, and for all that their coats got a good beating! Once Peter tried to see what he could do, but though some say that he is the prince of the apostles, under their handling he was reduced to being afraid of a sorry girl (Matt. 26:69–72).

'Besides, their king comes at their whistle. He's never out of hearing, and if at any time they are the worst for it, he can come in to help them. And it's said of him, "The sword that reaches him has no effect, nor does the spear or the dart or the javelin. Iron he treats like straw and bronze like rotten wood. Arrows do not make him flee; slingstones are like chaff to him. A club seems to him but a piece of straw; he laughs at the rattling of the lance" (Job 41:26–9). What can a man do in a case like this? It's true that if at every turn he could have Job's horse, and had skill and courage to ride him, he might do notable things. "Do you give the horse his strength or clothe his neck with a flowing mane? Do you make him leap like a locust, striking terror with his proud snorting? He paws fiercely, rejoicing in his strength, and charges into the fray. He laughs at fear, afraid of nothing; he does not shy away from the sword. The quiver rattles against his side, along with the flashing spear and lance. In frenzied excitement he eats up the ground; he cannot stand still when the trumpet sounds. At the blast of the trumpet he snorts, 'Aha!' He catches the scent of battle from afar, the shout of commanders and the battle cry" (Job 39:19–25).

'But as for footmen like you and me, don't let us ever want to meet such an enemy; nor boast as if we could do better when we hear of others who've been defeated; nor be tickled pink at the thought of our own bravery. People like that usually come off the worst when tried. Witness Peter, whom I referred to before. He'd swagger – yes, he would. In his conceit he maintained that he'd do better for his Master and stand up for him more than anybody else! But who was more defeated and overwhelmed by those villains than he was?

'When, therefore, we hear that robberies are committed on the King's highway, there are two things we'd better do. First, go out in armour, being certain to take a shield. It was because he had no shield that the man who laid in so heartily at Leviathan couldn't make him give in. Indeed, if we're without a shield, he's not at all afraid of us. That's why he who had skill said, "In addition to all this, take up the shield of faith, with which you can extinguish all the flaming arrows of the evil one" (Eph. 6:16).

'The second thing is to ask the King to give us a convoy – in fact, ask him to go with us himself. It was this that made David rejoice in the Valley of the Shadow of Death; and Moses was for dying where he stood rather than going one step without his God (Exod. 33:15). Oh, my brother, if he'll only go along with us, why need we be afraid of ten thousands who set themselves against us? But without him the proud helpers "fall among the slain" (Ps. 3:5–8; 27:1–3; Isa. 10:4).

'For my part,' continued Christian, 'I've been in the fray before now, and though, through the goodness of the One who is best, I am, as you see, still alive, I can't boast of my bravery. I'll be heartily glad if I don't meet any more such onslaughts, though I'm afraid we're not yet out of danger. However, since the lion and the bear haven't as yet devoured me (1 Sam. 17:34–7), I hope God will also deliver us from the next uncircumcised Philistine.'

Then Christian sang:

> Poor Little-faith! Hast been among the thieves?
> Wast robbed? Remember this, whoso believes,
> And get more faith, then shall you victors be
> Over ten thousand, else scarce over three.

So they went on, and Ignorance followed. They travelled like this till they came to a place where they saw another path join theirs. It seemed to lie as straight as the path they had to go along and they didn't know which of the two to take, for both seemed to go straight in front of them. They stood still to consider this and, as they were thinking, a man whose skin was black, but who was covered with a very light robe, came to them, and asked them why they were standing there. They answered that they were going to the Celestial City, but didn't know which path to take.

'Follow me,' said the man, 'that's where I'm going.'

So they followed him along the path, but now it led into a road, which turned round by degrees. It turned them so far from the city that they wished to go to that in a little while their faces were away from it. Yet still they followed him until before they realised it, he had led them both into a net, in which they became so entangled that they didn't know what to do. With that the white robe fell off the black man's back and they saw where they were. So there for some time they lay crying because they could't get themselves out.

Then Christian said to his companion, 'Now I see the mistake I've made. Didn't the shepherds tell us to beware of the Flatterer? Today we've found out the truth of the wise man's saying, "Whoever flatters his neighbour is spreading a net for his feet"' (Prov. 29:5).

Hopeful said, 'They also gave us written directions about the way, so we'd be more certain of finding it, but we've forgotten to read them, and have failed to keep ourselves from "the ways of the violent". David was wiser than we are, for he says, "As for the deeds of men – by the word of your lips, I have kept myself from the ways of the violent"' (Ps. 17:4).

So there they lay in the net, bewailing their plight. At last they spotted a Shining One coming towards them with a whip of small cords in his hand. When he reached them he asked them where they came from, and what they were doing there. They told him that they were poor pilgrims going to Zion, who had been led out of their way by a black man dressed in white.

'He told us to follow him,' they said, 'because he was going there, too.'

Then the one with the whip said, 'It is Flatterer, a false apostle, who is masquerading as an angel of light' (Prov. 19:5; 2 Cor. 11:13–15; Dan. 11:32). Then he tore the net, and let the men out. He said to them, 'Follow me, and I'll set you on your way again.' So he led them back to the path they'd left in order to follow the Flatterer. Then he asked them, 'Where did you sleep last night?'

'With the shepherds on the Delectable Mountains.'

He asked them then if the shepherds hadn't given them written directions of the route.

They answered, 'Yes.'

'But when you came to a standstill didn't you take them out and read them?'

'No.'

'Why not?'

'We forgot,' they replied.

He also asked them if the shepherds hadn't warned them to beware of the Flatterer?

They answered, 'Yes. But we didn't imagine that this well-spoken man would be he.' (Rom. 16:17–18)

Then I saw in my dream that he commanded them to lie down (Deut. 25:2), and when they did, he whipped them severely to teach them the good way they should walk (2 Chron. 6:26–7). And as he whipped them he said, 'Those whom I love I rebuke and discipline. So be earnest and repent' (Rev. 3:19). When this was done, he told them to go on their way, and pay careful attention to the other directions the shepherds had given them. So they thanked him for all his kindness, and went peacefully along the right way, singing:

> Come hither, you that walk along the way,
> See how the pilgrims fare that go astray.
> They catchèd are in an entangled net,
> 'Cause they good counsel lightly did forget.
> 'Tis true, they rescued were, but yet, you see,
> They're scourged to boot. Let this your caution be.

Now after a while they saw in the distance someone coming quietly by himself along the highway towards them. Then Christian said to his companion, 'Over there is a man with his back towards Zion, and he's coming to meet us.'

Atheist meets Christian and Hopeful

Hopeful said, 'I can see him. Let's be careful now in case he proves to be a flatterer as well.'

So the man, whose name was Atheist, came closer, and at last came up to them. 'Where're you going?' he asked.

'We're going to Mount Zion,' said Christian.

Then Atheist fell about laughing.

'What's the joke?' said Christian.

'I'm laughing at the sight of such ignoramuses – you've taken upon yourselves such a tedious journey, and yet you're likely to have nothing but your journey for your pains.'

'Why, man? Do you think we won't be accepted there?'

'Accepted! There's no such place as you dream of in all this world.'

'But there is in the world to come.'

'When I was at home in my own country I heard the same thing, and so I went out to see, and I've been seeking this city these twenty years, but have found no more of it than I did the first day I set out' (Eccles. 10:15; Jer. 22:12).

'We've both heard and believe that there is such a place,' protested Christian.

'If I hadn't believed it, too, when I was at home, I wouldn't have come so far to find it – but I've found no trace – and I would have, if there had been such a place, for I've gone farther than you. So I'm going back again, and I'll seek refreshment in the things that I cast away for the sake of what I now see is nothing at all.'

Then Christian said to Hopeful, 'Is what this man has said true?'

'Watch out,' said Hopeful, 'he's one of the flatterers. Remember what listening to that sort of fellow has cost us already! What! No Mount Zion! Didn't we see the gate of the city from the Delectable Mountains? And aren't we now told to walk by faith (2 Cor. 5:7)? Let's go on lest the man with the whip overtake us again. It's you who should have been teaching me this lesson, but I'll tell you roundly – "Stop listening to instruction, my son, and you will stray from the words of knowledge" (Prov. 19:27). I say, my brother, cease to hear him, and let us believe and be saved (Heb. 10:39).'

'Brother, I didn't ask you because I doubted what I believe, only to prove to you, and to draw out from you evidence of the honesty of your heart. As for this man, I know he's blinded by "the god of this age" (2 Cor. 4:4). Let's go on, knowing that we believe the truth, and "no lie comes from the truth" (1 John 2:21).'

'Now I "rejoice in the hope of the glory of God,"' Hopeful said. (Rom. 5:2)

So they turned away from the man, while he, still laughing at them, went on his way.

Then I saw in my dream, that they went on until they came to a country whose air tended to make any stranger feel very drowsy. Here Hopeful began to feel dull and heavy-headed. So he said to Christian, 'I'm beginning to grow so drowsy that I can scarcely keep my eyes open. Let's lie down here, and have a nap.'

'We absolutely mustn't,' said the other, 'in case we never wake up.'

'But why not? Sleep is sweet to the working man. If we have a nap we may be refeshed.'

'Don't you remember that one of the shepherds bade us beware of the Enchanted Ground? He meant that we should beware of sleeping. "So then, let us not be like others, who are asleep, but let us be alert and self-controlled"' (1 Thess. 5:6).

Then Hopeful admitted, 'I confess I'm in the wrong. And if I'd been here alone I'd have imperilled my life by sleeping. I see it's true what the wise man says, "Two are better than one" (Eccles. 4:9). Your company on this journey has been a blessing to me and you'll receive a good reward for your labour.'

'Now then,' said Christian, 'to stop ourselves falling asleep let's have a good discussion.'

'With all my heart,' said the other.

'Where shall we begin?'

'Where God began with us; but please, will you start?'

'First, I'll sing you this song,' Christian said.

> When saints do sleepy grow, let them come hither,
> And hear how these two pilgrims talk together.
> Yes, let them learn of them in any wise,
> Thus to keep ope their drowsy, slumbering eyes.
> Saints' fellowship, if it be managed well,
> Keeps them awake, and that in spite of hell.

Then Christian began. 'I'll ask you a question,' he said. 'What made you first think of doing what you're doing now?'

'Do you mean, how did I first come to care about the good of my soul?'

'Yes, that's what I meant.'

'Well, for a long time I continued to take great delight in all the things which were seen and sold at our fair, things which I now believe would have destroyed me in hell-fire if I'd kept on with them.'

'What things were they?' Christian asked.

Hopeful's life before conversion

'All the treasures and riches of the world. Also I took delight in rioting, orgies, wild parties, drinking, swearing, lying, promiscuity, Sabbath-breaking, and so on, that all lead to the destruction of the soul. But at last, through hearing and thinking about divine things – which, in fact, I heard about from you, and also from dear Faithful who was put to death in Vanity Fair for his faith and goodness – I found that "Those things result in death!" and that "because of such things God's wrath comes on those who are disobedient"' (Rom. 6:21–3; Eph. 5:6).

'And were you soon convicted?'

'No, at first I wasn't willing to recognise the evil of sin, nor the damnation that comes to those who commit it. When my mind first began to be disturbed by the word, I tried to shut my eyes against its light.'

'But what made you carry on like that when God's Spirit began to work in you?'

'The causes were:

'First, I didn't know that this was the work of God within me. I never thought that God begins the conversion of a sinner by making him aware of sin.

'Second, my body still found sin very sweet and I was loth to leave it.

'Third, I couldn't bring myself to break with my old companions. I very much liked being with them, and I liked everything they did.

'Fourth, the times when conviction of sin came on me were so upsetting and alarming that when they passed I couldn't bear even the memory of them.'

'So it seems that sometimes you got rid of your trouble?' commented Christian.

'Yes, certainly, but it would come back into my mind again, and then I'd feel as bad, in fact, worse than before.'

'Why, what was it that brought your sins to mind again?'

What brought back Hopeful's sense of sin

'Many things, such as:

1 If I simply met a good man in the streets, or,
2 If I heard anyone read from the Bible, or,
3 If my head began to ache, or,
4 If I heard that some of my neighbours were sick, or,
5 If I heard the bell toll for someone who had died, or,
6 If I thought of dying myself, or,
7 If I heard that sudden death had come to others.
8 But especially when I thought about myself, and that I must soon be brought before judgment.'

'And was it ever easy for you to throw off the guilt of sin when any of these things made it come over you?' asked Christian.

'No, not towards the end, for then they got a tighter grip on my conscience. And then, if I even thought about going back to my sin – though my mind had turned against it – the torment would be doubled.'

'And what did you do then?'

'I decided I must make an effort to put my life right, or else I thought I was certain to be damned.'

'And did you make the effort?'

'Yes, and I fled not only from my sins, but from sinful company, too, and took up religious duties, like praying, reading, weeping for sin, speaking the truth to my neighbours, etc. I did all these things, along with many others, too many to describe.'

'And then did you think you were all right?'

'Yes, for a while, but in the end all my misery came tumbling over me again, in spite of all my changes for the better.'

'How did that come about, since you were now a reformed man?'

Why reformation could not help

'Several things brought it on me, but especially sayings such as these: "all our righteous acts are like filthy rags"; "By observing the law no-one will be justified"; "when you have done everything you were told to do, [you] should say, 'We are unworthy servants'". (Isa. 64:6; Gal. 2:16; Luke 17:10). There were many more along the same lines. So I began to reason like this: if all my righteous acts are like filthy rags, if by observing the law no-one will be justified, and if, when we have done everything we are told to do we are still unworthy servants, then it's stupid to think keeping the law will get us to heaven. I also thought, if a man runs up a debt of a hundred pounds with a shopkeeper, but after that pays for everything he buys, his old debt still stands in the book. It's not been crossed out, and the shopkeeper may sue him, and have him thrown into prison till he can pay.'

'How did you apply this to yourself?'

'Why, I thought, "My sins have run a long way into God's book, and all my reforms won't pay off that score. Therefore, for all my recent improvements, I've still got to think how I can be set free from the damnation that I'm threatened with by my previous disobedience."'

'That's a good application,' Christian said, 'but please go on.'

'Another thing that worried me after I'd changed my ways was that if I looked carefully into even my best actions I could still see sin, new sin, mixing itself with the best of what I did. So I was forced to conclude that in spite of my earlier fancy ideas about myself and my duties, I'd committed enough sin in one duty to send me to hell, even if my former life had been faultless.'

'And what did you do then?'

'Do! I didn't know what to do till I unburdened myself to Faithful, for we knew each other well. He told me that unless I could get the righteousness of a man who had never sinned, neither my own righteousness, nor all the righteousness of the world, could save me.'

'And did you think he spoke the truth?'

'If he'd told me this when I was pleased and satisfied with the changes I'd made in my life, I'd have called him fool for his pains, but now, having seen my own weakness, and the sin which clung to my best efforts, I was forced to accept his opinion.'

'But when he first suggested it to you, did you think such a man could be found – someone who'd never committed any sin?'

'I must confess that at first the words sounded strange, but after spending a little more time talking to him, I was quite convinced.'

'And did you ask him who this man was, and how you could be put right by him?'

'Yes, and he told me it was the Lord Jesus, who dwells on the right hand of the Most High (Rom. 4; Col. 1; Heb. 10;

1 Pet. 3:22). "And this is how you can be justified, by him," he said. "It's by trusting in what he did by himself, when he was alive on earth, and suffered on the tree." I asked him how that man's righteousness could be powerful enough to justify someone else before God. And he told me he was the mighty God, and did what he did, and died, not for himself, but for me. And all the goodness of his life and actions would be set to my credit, if I believed on him.'

'And what did you do then?'

'I objected that he wouldn't be willing to save me.'

'And what did Faithful say to you then?'

'He told me to go to him and see. Then I said it would be presumptuous of me. But he said, "No, because you are invited to come" (Matt. 11:28). Then he gave me a book that Jesus had written to encourage me and make me feel more free to come. And he said, "The smallest letter, and the least stroke of a pen in that book remain firmer than heaven and earth" (Matt. 24:35; 5:18). Then I asked him what I must do when I came. And he told me that on my knees, and with all my heart and soul, I must entreat the Father to reveal Jesus to me (Ps. 95:6; Jer. 29:12–13; Dan. 6:10). Then I asked him how I must make my prayer. And he said, "Go, and you'll find him on a mercy seat, where he sits all the year long, to give pardon and forgiveness to those who come." I told him that I didn't know what to say when I came (Exod. 25:22; Lev. 16:2; Num. 7:8–9; Heb. 4:16). And he told me to speak as follows: "God, be merciful to me a sinner", and "Make me know and believe in Jesus Christ. For I see that if his righteousness had never come to us, or if I don't have faith in that righteousness, I'm utterly cast away. Lord, I've heard that you are a merciful God, and have ordained that your Son Jesus Christ should be the Saviour of the world, and that you are willing to bestow him on such a poor sinner as I am – and I'm a sinner indeed. Therefore, Lord, take this opportunity, and reveal your grace in the salvation of my soul, through your Son Jesus Christ. Amen."'

'And did you do as you were told?' asked Christian.

'Yes, over and over again.'

'And did the Father reveal the Son to you?'

'Not the first time, nor the second, or third, or fourth, or fifth. Not the sixth time either.'

'What did you then?'

'What! I just didn't know what to do.'

'Didn't you think about not praying?'

'Yes, a hundred times over.'

'And why didn't you stop?'

'I believed that what I had been told was true – that without the righteousness of this Christ all the world couldn't save me. So, I thought to myself, if I stop I die, and I might as well die at the throne of grace. Moreover these words came into my mind: "Though it linger, wait for it; it will certainly come and will not delay" (Hab. 2:3). So I continued praying until the Father showed me his Son.'

'And how was he revealed to you?'

How Christ was revealed to Hopeful

'I didn't see him with my physical eyes, but with the eyes of my heart (Eph. 1:18–19). It was like this: one day I was very sad, I think sadder than at any time in my life, and this sadness was the result of a fresh sight of the greatness and vileness of my sins. I was expecting nothing but hell, and the everlasting damnation of my soul. But suddenly I thought I saw the Lord Jesus looking down from heaven on me and saying, "Believe in the Lord Jesus, and you will be saved" (Acts 16:31). I replied, "Lord, I'm a great, a very great sinner." And he answered, "My grace is sufficient for you" (2 Cor. 12:9). But I said, "But, Lord, what is believing?" And then I understood from the words, "He who comes to me will never be hungry, and he who believes in me will never be thirsty" (John 6:35) that believing and coming are all one. So someone who comes, that is, who runs out in his heart and feelings after salvation by Christ, is someone who believes in Christ. Then my eyes filled with tears and I asked, "But, Lord, will you really accept and save such a great sinner as I am?" 'And I heard him say, "whoever comes to me I will never drive away" (John 6:37).

Then I said, "But how, Lord, must I think of you as I come to you, so that I may trust you in the right way?" Then he said, "Christ Jesus came into the world to save sinners" (1 Tim. 1:15). "Christ is the end of the law so that there may be righteousness for everyone who believes" (Rom. 10:4). "He was delivered over to death for our sins and was raised to life for our justification" (Rom. 4:25). "[He] loves us and has freed us from our sins by his blood" (Rev. 1:5). "He is the mediator" (Heb. 9:15) between God and us. "Because Jesus lives for ever, he has a permanent priesthood" (Heb. 7:24–5). From all this I gathered that I must look for righteousness in his person, and for forgiveness of my sins by his blood; and that what he did when he obeyed his Father's law, and submitted to the law's penalty, was not for himself, but for anyone who will, in thankfulness, accept it for his salvation. And now my heart was full of joy, my eyes full of tears, and my feelings running over with love to the name of Jesus Christ, to his people, and all his ways.'

Then Christian said, this was indeed a revelation of Christ to your soul. But tell me how this particularly affected your spirit.'

'It made me see that all the world, in spite of the goodness in it, is in a state of condemnation. It made me see how God the Father, though he is just, can with justice justify the sinner who comes to him. It made me feel very ashamed of the evil of my former life, and I was overwhelmed with a sense of my own ingorance, for up till then not one thought had come to my heart to show me the beauty of Jesus Christ. It made me love a holy life, and long to do something for the honour and glory of the name of the Lord Jesus. Itrhoguht that if I had a thousand gallons of blood in my body I could spill it all for the sake of the Lord Jesus.'

18

Ignorance

Then in my dream I saw that Hopeful looked back, and saw
Ignorance, whom they had left behind, coming after them.
'Look how far that youngster is lagging behind,' he said to
Christian.

'Yes, I can see him. He doesn't fancy our company.'

'But I reckon it wouldn't have hurt him to have kept up
with us.'

'That's true. But I bet you he thinks differently.'

'I bet he does. All the same, let's wait for him.'

So they did.

Then Christian said to Ignorance, 'Come on, man, why
are you keeping so far behind?'

'I'm much happier walking alone than in company –
unless I like it better,' Ignorance said.

Then Christian whispered to Hopeful, 'Didn't I tell you
he doesn't care for our company? But, come on, let's talk
the time away in this solitary place.' Then, addressing
Ignorance, he said, 'Well, how are you? How are things
between God and your soul now?'

'Fine, I hope, for I'm always full of good ideas that come
into my mind and encourage me as I walk along.'

'What good ideas? Please, do tell us,' Christian said.

'Why, I think of God and heaven.'

'So do the devils and damned souls.'

'But I think of them and desire them.'

'So do many who are never likely to come there. "The
sluggard craves and gets nothing"' (Prov. 13:4).

'But I think of them, and have left everything for them.'

'I doubt that. It's very hard to leave everything – far harder than many people realise. What makes you think you've left everything for God and heaven?'

'My heart tells me so.'

'The wise man says, "He who trusts in himself is a fool" (Prov. 28:26).

'That refers to an evil heart, but mine is a good one.'

'How can you prove that?' Christian asked.

'It comforts me in the hope of heaven,' said Ignorance.

'That may be through its deceitfulness. A man's heart may minister comfort to him by offering hope when there are no grounds for hoping.'

'But my heart and life agree together, and therefore my hope is well grounded.'

'Who told you that your heart and life agree together?'

'My heart tells me.'

'"Ask my companion if I'm a thief!" Your heart tells you! Any testimony is useless unless the word of God backs it up.'

'But isn't a heart good, if it has good thoughts? And isn't a life good when it's lived according to God's commandments?'

'Yes, a heart is good if it has good thoughts, and a life is good if it's lived according to God's commandments, but it's one thing to *have* these, and quite another only to *think* you have them.'

'Well, tell me – what do you count as good thoughts and a life lived according to God's commandments?'

'There are different sorts of good thoughts: thoughts about ourselves, about God, about Christ, and about other things.'

'What are good thoughts about ourselves?'

'Thoughts that agree with the word of God.'

'When do our thoughts about ourselves agree with the word of God?'

'When we pass the same judgment upon ourselves that

the word passes. The word of God says about people in their natural state: "There is no-one righteous, not even one" (Rom. 3:10). It also says that "every inclination of the thoughts of his [man's] heart was only evil all the time" (Rom. 3; Gen. 6:5). And again, "every inclination of his heart is evil from childhood" (Gen. 8:21). Now, when we think like that about ourselves, and feel it, then our thoughts are good ones, because they accord with the word of God,' Christian said.

'I'll never believe that my heart is so bad.'

'Therefore you've never had one good thought about yourself in all your life! But let me go on. Just as the word passes a judgment on our hearts, so it passes a judgment on our conduct, and when our thoughts about our hearts and our conduct agree with the judgment which the word gives about them, then they're good.'

'Explain what you mean.'

'Why, the word of God says that men's ways are crooked ways – not good, they're perverse. It says that by nature men are not on the good way, they've not known it (Ps. 125:5; Prov. 2:15; Rom. 3:17). Now when a man thinks that about his ways, when he consciously and with a sense of deep humility thinks like that, then he has good thoughts about his ways, because his thoughts now agree with the judgment of the word of God.'

'What are good thoughts about God?'

'As I've said about ourselves, they are when our thoughts about God agree with what the word says about him, that is, when we think of his being and attributes as the word teaches us. I can't talk now about that in general, but with reference to us, then we have right thoughts about God when we think that he knows us better than we know ourselves, and can see sin in us when and where we can see none; when we think he knows our inmost thoughts, and that our heart, with all its depths, is always open to him; also when we think that all our righteousness stinks in his nostrils, and therefore that before him we cannot be confident of anything at all, not even of all our best efforts.'

'Do you think that I'm such a fool as to think that God can see no farther than I can? Or that I'd come to God relying on even the best of my efforts?' protested Ignorance.

'Well, what do you think, then?' asked Christian.

'Why, in short, I think I must believe in Christ for justification.'

'What! Think you must believe in Christ, when you don't see that you need him? You can neither see your original nor your present infirmities. Your high opinion of yourself, and of what you do, plainly indicates that you're someone who's never seen any need for Christ's personal righteousness to justify you before God. So how can you say you believe in Christ?'

'I believe well enough for all that.'

'How do you believe?'

'I believe that Christ died for sinners, and that I'll be justified before God and set free from the curse, when he graciously accepts my obedience to his law. Put it like this: Christ, because of his goodness, makes the religious duties I perform acceptable to his Father. And so I'll be justified.'

'Let me give an answer to this statement of your faith,' Christian said.

'1 Your faith is a fantasy – it's not the sort of faith that's described anywhere in the word of God.

'2 Your faith is false because justification no longer depends on the personal righteousness of Christ but on your own righteousness.

'3 Your faith makes Christ justify your actions, and you for the sake of your actions, which is false.

'4 Therefore your faith is deceitful, and will leave you still under the wrath of God in the day of God Almighty. For true justifying faith sends the soul – which is keenly aware of its lost condition under the law – flying for refuge to Christ's righteousness. And this righteousness is not an act of grace which justifies your obedience and makes it acceptable to God, but it is his personal obedience to the law. He did and suffered for us everything that the law required us to do. As I say, it is this righteousness which true faith accepts. The soul sheltering under the skirt of this righteousness is presented spotless before God. Therefore God accepts it and acquits it.'

'What!' exclaimed Ignorance. 'Would you have us trust to what Christ in his own person has done, without our doing anything at all? This fanciful idea will loosen the reins holding our passions, and set us free to live as we wish. What does it matter how we live, if we can be justified by believing in Christ's personal righteousness?'

'Ignorance is your name, and that's what you are,' said Christian. 'This answer proves it. You're ignorant of what justifying righteousness is, and just as ignorant about how faith can save your soul from the heavy wrath of God. And you're ignorant about the true results of this saving faith. It means when the heart is won over to God in Christ, and bows to him. You love his name, his word, his ways, and people. It's not as you ignorantly imagine.'

'Ask him if Christ was ever revealed to him from heaven,' put in Hopeful.

'What!' exclaimed Ignorance. 'You're for revelations! I really believe that what you and all the rest of you say about that is the result of a disordered mind.'

'Why, man!' Hopeful said. 'Christ is so hidden in God from man's natural understanding that no one can know him in a saving way unless God the Father reveals him.'

'That's your faith, but not mine. I've no doubt that mine is as good as yours, though I don't have as many fancy ideas in my head as you do.'

'Let me say something,' Christian interrupted. 'You ought not to be so quick to dismiss this subject. I'll come right out and say, as my good friend has already said, that no one can know Jesus Christ unless he has a revelation from the Father. Yes, and faith too, which, if it's a right faith, is how the soul holds on to Christ. That faith is created in us by the extraordinary greatness of his mighty power (Matt. 11:27; 1 Cor. 12:3; Eph. 1:18–19). But, poor Ignorance, I can see you're ignorant about how this faith works. Wake up. Look at the wretched state you're in and fly to the Lord Jesus. By his righteousness, which is the righteousness of God – since he himself is God – you'll be delivered from condemnation.'

'You're walking too quickly,' Ignorance said, 'I can't keep up with you. Go on ahead. I'll have to stay behind for a while.'

Then they said:

> Well, Ignorance, wilt thou yet foolish be,
> To slight good counsel, ten times given thee?
> And, if thou yet refuse it, thou shalt know,
> Ere long, the evil of thy doing so.
> Remember, man, in time; stoop, do not fear,
> Good counsel taken will save; therefore hear.
> But, if thou yet shalt slight it, thou wilt be
> The loser, Ignorance, I'll warrant thee.

Then Christian said to his companion: 'Well, come on, Hopeful, I see that you and I are walking by ourselves again.'

So in my dream I saw that they went on ahead as before, while Ignorance came hobbling behind. Then Christian said to his companion, 'I really pity this poor man. Things will go badly for him at the end.'

'Yes,' agreed Hopeful. 'Unfortunately there are lots of people in our town in his condition – whole families, whole streets in fact, and pilgrims, too. And if there are so many around me, how many do you think there must be where he was born?'

'Indeed, the word says, "He has blinded their eyes so they cannot see,"' said Christian. 'But now we're by ourselves, what do you think of such people? Do you think they've never been convicted of sin, and the danger they're in?'

'Hold on – why don't you answer that question yourself, since you're older than I am.'

'Then I say that I think they sometimes may be. But being naturally ignorant they don't understand that such convictions are for their good. Therefore they seek desperately to stifle them, and in their presumption continue to flatter themselves about the state of their own hearts.'

The good use of fear

Hopeful nodded. 'I do believe, as you say, that fear tends to do people a lot of good. At the beginning it puts them in the right frame of mind to go on a pilgrimage.'

'Without any doubt it does, if it is a right fear, for that's what the word says, "The fear of the Lord is the beginning of knowledge"' (Job 28:28; Ps. 111:10; Prov. 1:7; 9:10).

'How would you describe a right fear?'

'*True* or *right* fear is revealed by three things:

'1 By its rise: it's caused by a saving conviction of sin.

'2 It drives the soul to hold fast to Christ for salvation.

'3 It generates and fosters in the soul a great reverence for God, for his word and ways. It keeps the soul sensitive, and makes it afraid to turn to the right hand or to the left. It stops the soul doing anything that may dishonour God, destroy its peace, grieve the Spirit, or give the enemy cause to insult us.'

'Well said. I believe you've spoken the truth. Are we almost past the Enchanted Ground now?'

'Why? Are you tired of this conversation?' asked Christian.

'No, honestly, but I wondered where we are.'

Why ignorant people stifle convictions

'We've no more than two miles to go. But let's return to our subject. Now people who are ignorant don't know that convictions which tend to make them afraid are for their good. So they try to stifle them.'

'How do they seek to stifle them?'

'First,' said Christian, 'they think that those fears come from the devil (though actually they come from God), and, thinking that, they resist them as if they were directly aimed at their downfall.

'Second, they also think that these fears tend to harm their faith, when, sad to say, the poor men have no faith at all! And therefore they harden their hearts against their fears.

'Third, they presume that they ought not to feel fear, and therefore, in spite of their fears, they grow arrogantly confident.

'Fourth, they realise that those fears tend to take away from them their pitiful old feeling of personal holiness, and therefore they do all they can to resist them.'

'I know something of this myself,' agreed Hopeful, 'for before I knew myself that's how it was with me.'

'Well, for the time being let's leave our neighbour Ignorance to himself, and look at another helpful question.'

'With all my heart. But will you still begin?'

'Well, then, about ten years ago, did you know someone called Temporary who lived in your area? In those days he was a prominent man in religious affairs.'

'Know him! Yes, he lived in Graceless, a town about two miles off Honesty, and he lived next door to Turnback.'

'Right, they dwelt under the same roof. Well, that man was once very alive to spiritual things. I believe that he saw something of his sin, and of the wages that were its due.'

'I think so, too. My house was not more than three miles from his and he'd often come to see me in tears. Honestly, I felt sorry for him, and had some hope for him. But you can see that it's not everyone who cries, "Lord, Lord."'

'He told me once that he'd resolved to go on a pilgrimage – like us now. But all of a sudden he got to know Saveself, and then he didn't want to know me.'

'Well, since we're talking about him, let's look into the reason for his sudden backsliding and that of others like him.'

'It may be very helpful, but you begin,' said Christian.

'Well, then, in my judgment there are four reasons.

'First: though the consciences of such men are stirred, their minds are not changed. Therefore, when the power of guilt wears away, the feeling that provoked them into becoming religious ceases. So they naturally return to their former way of life. It's like a dog whose food has made him sick. As long as the sickness lasts he keeps vomiting up all his food: not because he's decided to do this from a free mind – if we can say a dog has a mind – but because he's got an upset stomach, he doesn't dislike the vomit itself. So when his stomach is better he turns around and licks up all the sick. Therefore, what is written is true – "A dog returns to its vomit" (2 Pet. 2:22). In the same way, they're on fire for heaven only because of their awareness and fear of the torments of hell. As their sense of hell and their fear of damnation chills and cools, their desire for heaven and salvation cools, too. And eventually, when their guilt and fear are gone, their desire for heaven and happiness dies, and they return to their old course.

'Second: another reason is that they're controlled by slavish fears. I mean, they're afraid of people. "Fear of man will prove to be a snare" (Prov. 29:25). So, then, as long as the flames of hell are about their ears they seem to be on fire for heaven. But when that terror has passed, they have second thoughts. They think that it's better to be wise, and not to run the risk of losing everything – or at the very least not to risk bringing themselves into unavoidable and unnecessary troubles for who knows what. And so they fall in with the world again.

'Third: the disgrace that accompanies religion blocks their way. They're proud and haughty, and in their eyes religion is low and contemptible. Therefore, when they've

lost their sense of hell and of the wrath to come, they return
to their former way of life.

'Fourth: they find guilt and thinking about terror very
upsetting. They don't like seeing their misery before they
reach it. Possibly their first sight of it – if they'd accepted
that sight – might have made them fly to where the righteous run and are safe. But because, as I suggested earlier,
they shun the very thought of guilt and terror, as soon as
they're rid of their premonitions about the terrors and
wrath of God, they gladly harden their hearts, and choose
ways that'll harden them more and more.'

Christian agreed. 'You're close to the nub of the matter,'
he said. 'When it comes down to it, their minds and will
haven't changed. They're like the criminal standing in front
of the judge who shivers and shakes, and seems to repent
most sincerely, but who's motivated by his fear of the noose
not by hatred of his offence. Only let this man have his freedom back, and he'll be a thief and hooligan again, whereas
if his mind had changed, he'd be different.'

'Now I've shown you why they go back, so will you show
me how they do it,' suggested Hopeful.

How the apostate gets back

'Gladly,' said Christian.

'1 As far as they can they stop thinking about God,
death, and judgment.

'2 Then bit by bit they neglect private religious practices,
like a personal prayer-time, curbing their lusts, watchful-
ness, sorrow for sin, and so on.

'3 Then they shun the company of lively and warm
Christians.

'4 After that they became indifferent to public religious
duties, like hearing and reading God's word, fellowship
with other Christians, and so on.

'5 They then begin to pick holes, so to speak, in the coats of Christian people, doing it for devilish purposes so that, just because of some weakness they've spotted in other Christians, they can blacken religion behind their backs.

'6 Then they begin to associate with worldly, undisciplined, and unprincipled people.

'7 Then in secret they indulge in worldly and lewd talk and are only too glad if they can see evidence of such conduct in supposedly upright people, to encourage them in their own wrongdoing.

'8 After this they begin to play with little sins openly.

'9 And then, thoroughly hardened, they show themselves as they are. Launched once again into the chasm of misery, they for ever perish in their own deceptions, unless they are shaped by a miracle of grace.'

19

The Land of Beulah
– The Fords of the River –
At-Home

Now in my dream I saw that by this time the pilgrims had
left the Enchanted Ground and were entering the land of
Beulah (Isa. 62:4), where the air was very sweet and pleasant. As the path led through this land they were able to
refresh themselves there for a time. There they continually
heard the singing of birds, and every day saw the flowers
appear on the earth, and heard the cooing of doves (S. of S.
2:12) in the land. In this country the sun shines night and
day, for this land is beyond the Valley of the Shadow of
Death, and out of the reach of Giant Despair, nor could
they as much as see Doubting Castle. They were within
sight of the city they were going to, and also met some of its
inhabitants, for this land is on the borders of heaven and the
Shining Ones frequently walk in it. It was in this land that
the contract between the Bride and the Bridegroom was
renewed: yes, 'as a bridegroom rejoices over his bride, so
will your God rejoice over you' (Isa. 62:5). There they
lacked neither corn nor wine, for they found plenty of
everything they had looked for in all their pilgrimage.
There they heard voices from out of the City – loud voices,
saying, 'Say to the Daughter of Zion, "See, your Saviour
comes! See, his reward is with him, and his recompense
accompanies him"' (Isa. 62:11). And all the inhabitants of
the country called them 'the Holy People, the Redeemed of
the Lord . . . [the] Sought After' (Isa. 62:12).

As they walked in this land they were far happier than they had been in places more remote from the kingdom to which they were bound, and being closer to the City they had an even finer view of it. It was built of pearls and precious stones, and its streets were paved with gold. When he saw the natural glory of the City, and the reflection of the sun shining on it, Christian fell sick with desire. Hopeful also had several attacks of the same illness. So here they lay for a while, crying out because of their pangs, 'If you find my lover, what will you tell him? Tell him I am faint with love' (S. of S. 5:8).

But at last, feeling a little stronger, and more able to bear their sickness, they continued on their way, and came nearer and nearer to the city. Here there were orchards, vineyards, and gardens with gates which opened straight on to the highway. As they came up to these places they saw the gardener standing on the path. The pilgrims said to him, 'Whose lovely vineyards and gardens are these?'

He answered, 'They are the King's, and are planted here for his own pleasure, and also for the refreshment of pilgrims.'

So the gardener led them into the vineyards, and told them to refresh themselves with the delicious fruit (Deut. 23:24). He also showed them the King's walks and the arbours where he delighted to go, and here they lingered and slept.

Now in my dream I saw that at this time they talked more in their sleep than in all their journey so far. As I was wondering about this the gardener spoke to me. 'Why are you wondering about this? The grapes of these vineyards "goeth down sweetly, causing the lips of them that are asleep to speak"' (S. of S. 7:9 AV).

I saw that when they were awake they got ready to go up to the City. But, as I said, the reflection of the sun on the City (for the City was 'of pure gold' [Rev. 21:18]), was so gloriously brilliant that as yet they could not look openly at it, but could only look through an instrument made for that purpose. Then I saw that as they went on they were met by two men. Their clothes shone like gold, and their faces shone like the light (2 Cor. 3:18).

These men asked the pilgrims where they came from, and they told them. They also asked them where they had lodged, and what difficulties and dangers, what encouragements and pleasures, they had met on the way, and they told them. Then the men who met them said, 'You have only two difficulties to overcome, and then you're in the City.'

Christian and his companion asked the men to go along with them, and they told them that they would. 'But,' they said, 'you must reach the City by your own faith.'

I saw in my dream that they went on together till they came within sight of the gate, but then I saw that between them and the gate there was a river. The river was very deep and there was no bridge over it. At the sight of this river the pilgrims were stunned but the men with them said, 'You must go through, or you cannot come to the gate.'

Death is not welcome to nature, though by it we pass out of this world into glory

The pilgrims then asked if there was no other way to the gate. The men answered, 'Yes, but since the foundation of the world only two people – Enoch and Elijah – have been permitted to tread that path. Nor will anyone else go along it until the last trumpet sounds' (1 Cor. 15:51–2). At this these pilgrims, and especially Christian, began to feel very despondent. They looked this way and that but could find no way to avoid the river. Then they asked the men if the river was the same depth right the way across. They said, 'No, it's not. But this won't help you. You'll find it deeper or shallower according to your trust in the King.'

So they prepared to face the water. As he waded in, Christian began to sink. Crying out to his good friend Hopeful, he said, 'I'm sinking in deep waters; the breakers are going over my head, all the waves are going over me. Selah.'

Christian's conflict at the hour of death

Then Hopeful said, 'Cheer up, brother; I can feel the bottom, and it's good.'

But Christian called out, 'Oh! my friend, "The sorrows of death have compassed me about." I shall not see the land that flows with milk and honey.' And with that a great darkness and horror fell on Christian so that he was unable to see ahead. Also he lost most of his senses, so that he could neither remember nor talk correctly about any of the sweet encouragements that he had received during his pilgrimage. Everything he said revealed that his mind was full of horror, and his heart full of dread. He was terrified that he would die in that river and never go through the gate. Those who stood watching also saw that he was obsessed by thoughts of the sins that he'd committed, both before and after he had become a pilgrim. From time to time his words revealed that he was also troubled by apparitions of hobgoblins and evil spirits.

Hopeful had great difficulty in keeping his brother's head above water, in fact sometimes Christian went quite under and then after a while would rise up again half dead.

Hopeful tried to comfort him, saying, 'Brother, I can see the gate, and men standing by it to receive us.'

But Christian would answer, 'It's you, it's you they're waiting for, you've been hopeful ever since I've known you.'

'And so have you,' Hopeful said.

'Oh, brother, surely if I were right with God he'd come to help me, but he's brought me into this snare, because of my sins and has left me.'

Then Hopeful said, 'My brother, you've quite forgotten that text about the wicked which says: "They have no struggles; their bodies are healthy and strong. They are free from the burdens common to man; they are not plagued by human ills" (Ps. 73:4–5). The troubles and distresses you're going through are not a sign that God has forsaken you. They're sent to try you, to see whether you'll call to mind all you've experienced up to now of his goodness, and dwell upon him in your distress.'

Christian delivered from his fear of death

Then I saw in my dream that Christian was lost in thought for a while. Then Hopeful added these words, 'Be of good cheer, Jesus Christ makes you whole.'

With that Christian broke out with a loud cry, 'Oh, I see him again! And he tells me, "When you pass through the waters, I will be with you; and when you pass through the rivers, they will not sweep over you"' (Isa. 43:2).

Then they both took courage, and after that the enemy was as still as a stone until they had gone over. Soon Christian found ground to stand on, and after that the rest of the river was only shallow. So they got over.

Now on the bank of the river on the far side they saw the two shining men again, waiting for them. As they came out of the river the men saluted them, and said, 'We are ministering spirits sent to serve those who will inherit salvation' (Heb. 1:14). In this way they went along towards the gate.

Now you must note that the city stood on a great hill. But the pilgrims went up that hill easily because these two men were holding their arms and leading them. Also they had left their earthly clothes behind them in the river, for though they went in wearing them, they came out without them. Therefore they went up quickly and nimbly, though the foundation upon which the city was built was higher than the clouds. So they went up through the regions of the air, talking delightedly as they went, feeling very encouraged because they were over the river, and were accompanied by such glorious companions.

The conversation was about the glory of the place. The Shining Ones told Christian and Hopeful that no words could express its beauty and glory. 'There,' they said, 'is Mount Zion, the heavenly Jerusalem . . . thousands upon thousands of angels . . . the spirits of righteous men made perfect' (Heb. 12:22–23). 'You are going now,' they said, 'to the Paradise of God, where you will see the Tree of Life, and eat its never-fading fruits. And when you arrive white robes will be given you, and every day you will walk and talk with the King, even all the days of eternity (Rev. 2:7; 3:4–5; 22:5). You will never see again the things you saw when you were in the lower regions upon the earth – sorrow, sickness, and death, for the former things are passed away (Isa. 65:16). You are going now to Abraham, to Isaac and Jacob, and to the prophets, men whom God has taken away from the evil to come, and who are now resting on their beds, each one walking in his righteousness' (Isa. 57:1–2).

Christian and Hopeful then asked, 'What must we do in the holy place?'

And they were told, 'There you will receive comfort for all your toil, and joy for all your sorrow. You will reap what you have sown, even the fruit of all your prayers, your tears, and sufferings for the King as you came on your way (Gal. 6:7–8). In that place you will wear crowns of gold, and always enjoy the sight and vision of the Holy One, for there you "shall see him as he is" (1 John 3:2). There also you will serve him continually with praise and shouting and thanksgiving. You will serve the One you longed to serve in the world though you found it so difficult because of the weakness of your flesh. There your eyes will be delighted with seeing, and your ears with hearing the pleasant voice of the Mighty One. There you will enjoy your friends again, who have gone there before you, and there you will receive with joy everyone who follows you into the holy place. There also you will be clothed with glory and majesty, and put into a carriage fit to ride out with the King of Glory. When he comes with sound of the trumpet in the clouds, as upon the wings of the wind, you will come with him, and when he sits upon the throne of judgment you will sit by him. Yes, and when he passes sentence upon all evil-doers, be they angels or men, you will also have a voice in that judgment, because they are his and your enemies. Also, when he again returns to the city, you will go, too, with the sound of trumpet, and be with him for ever' (1 Thess. 4:13–17; Jude 14; Dan. 7:9–10; 1 Cor. 6:2–3).

Now while they were drawing close to the gate, a company of the heavenly host came out to meet them. The two Shining Ones said: 'These are the men who loved our Lord when they were in the world, and have left everything for his holy name. He has sent us to fetch them and we have brought them up to here on their longed-for journey so that they may go in and look at their Redeemer with joy.'

Then the heavenly host gave a great shout, saying, 'Blessed are those who are invited to the wedding supper of the Lamb' (Rev. 19:9). Several of the King's trumpeters also came to meet them, clothed in white and shining garments, and all the heavens echoed to the sound of their melodious notes. These trumpeters greeted Christian and his companion with ten thousand welcomes from the world, saluting them with shouting and trumpet call.

After this the company surrounded them on every side. Some went before, some behind, some on the right hand, and some on the left as if to guard them through the upper regions. As they went the melodious music rang out on high, so that to those watching it was as if heaven itself had come down to meet them. In this way they walked on together, and as they walked every now and then these trumpeters, with joyful notes, with music and looks and gestures, still showed to Christian and his brother how welcome they were in that company, and with what gladness they had come to meet them.

And now it was as if Christian and Hopeful were in heaven before they reached it. They were swallowed up with the sight of angels, and the sound of their melodious notes. All this time they could see the city itself and they thought they could hear all the bells in the city ringing out to welcome them in. But, above all, they were filled with warm and joyful thoughts about how they would live there with such company, for ever and ever. Oh what tongue, or pen, could express their glorious joy! And so in this way they came up to the gate.

Now when they arrived there they saw written over it in letters of gold the words, 'Blessed are those who wash their robes, that they may have right to the tree of life, and may go through the gates into the city' (Rev 22:14).

Then in my dream I saw that the shining men bade them call at the gate. When they had done this some from above looked over the gate – Enoch, Moses, and Elijah, with others. They were told, 'These pilgrims have come from the city of Destruction, because of their love for the King of this place.'

And then each pilgrim gave in the certificate which he had received at the beginning. These were carried to the King, who, when he had read them, said, 'Where are the men?'

He was told, 'They are standing outside the gate.'

'Open the gates,' commanded the King, 'that the righteous nation may enter, the nation that keeps faith' (Isa. 26:2).

Now in my dream I saw that these two men went in at the gate. And behold, as they entered, they were transfigured, and garments were put on them that shone like gold. Others met them with harps and crowns, which they gave to them. The harps were for praise, the crowns were in token of honour. Then I heard in my dream that all the bells in the city rang out again for joy, and the pilgrims were told, 'Come and share your master's happiness!' (Matt. 25:21).

I also heard Christian and Hopeful singing aloud and saying, "To him who sits on the throne and to the Lamb be praise and honour and glory and power, for ever and ever!" (Rev. 5:13).

Just as the gates were opened to let in the men, I looked in after them. The city shone like the sun, the streets were paved with gold, and in the streets walked many men with crowns on their heads. They had palms in their hands, and carried golden harps with which to sing praises.

Some had wings, and they spoke to one another saying, 'Holy, holy, holy, is the Lord!'

After that they shut the gates. And I was outside, wishing I were among them.

Now while I was gazing at all these things I turned my head to look back, and saw Ignorance come up to the riverside. He got over quickly and without half the difficulty which the other two had experienced, for as it happened a ferryman, called Vain-hope had come, and with his boat had helped him over. So Ignorance, like the others, climbed the hill to come up to the gate, only he came alone, and no one met him with the least encouragement. When he arrived at the gate he looked up to the writing that was above it and then began to knock, supposing that he would be quickly admitted. But the man who looked over the top of the gate asked him, 'Where are you from and what do you want?'

He answered, 'I've eaten and drunk in the presence of the King, and he has taught in our streets.'

Then they asked him for his certificate so that they might go and show it to the King. He fumbled in his clothes for one, and found none.

Then said they, 'Haven't you got one?' But the man was silent. So they told the King, but he wouldn't come down to see him. Instead he commanded the two Shining Ones who had conducted Christian and Hopeful to the City, to go out and take Ignorance, and bind him hand and foot, and lead him away. They took him up, and carried him through the air to a door in the side of the hill, and put him there. Then I saw that there was a way to hell even from the gates of heaven, as well as from the City of Destruction. So I awoke, and saw it was a dream.

Conclusion

Now, reader, I have told my dream to thee,
See if thou canst interpret it to me,
Or to thyself, or neighbour: but take heed
Of misinterpreting; for that, instead
Of doing good, will but thyself abuse:
By misinterpreting, evil ensues.

Take heed also that thou be not extreme
In playing with the outside of my dream;
Nor let my figure or similitude
Put thee into a laughter or a feud.
Leave this for boys and fools; but as for thee,
Do thou the substance of my matter see.

Put by the curtains, look within the veil,
Turn up my metaphors, and do not fail.
There, if thou seekest them, such things thou'lt find
As will be helpful to an honest mind.

What of my dross thou findest there, be bold
To throw away, but yet preserve the gold.
What if my gold be wrapped up in ore?
None throws away the apple for the core;
But if thou shalt cast all away as vain,
I know not but 'twill make me dream again.

Index to Bible References

General Index